Power Manifesting

ALSO BY PAUL McKENNA

Success for Life: The Secret to Achieving Your True Potential

Freedom from Anxiety

Positivity: Confidence, Resilience, Motivation

Power Manifesting

The New Science of
Getting What You Want

PAUL McKENNA DPhil

Copyright © Paul McKenna 2025

The right of Paul McKenna to be identified as the Author of the Work has been asserted by him in accordance with the Copyright, Designs and Patents Act 1988.

First published in 2025 by Headline Welbeck Non-Fiction
An imprint of Headline Publishing Group Limited

Apart from any use permitted under UK copyright law, this publication may only be reproduced, stored, or transmitted, in any form, or by any means, with prior permission in writing of the publishers or, in the case of reprographic production, in accordance with the terms of licences issued by the Copyright Licensing Agency.

Cataloguing in Publication Data is available from the British Library

Trade Paperback ISBN 9781035428298

Illustrations by Ben Hasler, NB Illustration

Typeset in Sabon Next by seagulls.net

Printed and bound in Great Britain by Clays Ltd, Elcograf S.p.A.

Headline's policy is to use papers that are natural, renewable and recyclable products and made from wood grown in sustainable forests. The logging and manufacturing processes are expected to conform to the environmental regulations of the country of origin.

Headline Publishing Group Limited
An Hachette UK Company
Carmelite House
50 Victoria Embankment
London EC4Y 0DZ

The authorised representative in the EEA is Hachette Ireland,
8 Castlecourt Centre, Dublin 15, D15 XTP3, Ireland (email: info@hbgi.ie)

www.headline.co.uk
www.hachette.co.uk

This book and audio programmes are intended for educational change. If you suspect you are suffering from a psychiatric disorder, contact your physician.

Important Note

These pages contain powerful, scientific, physical and psychological techniques that will enable you to get clear about what you want in life and how to manifest it. But this book is only half of what you need. The other half is a series of powerful audio techniques that will help you programme your unconscious mind, so you can focus like a laser beam on creating the life you want.

These can be found at www.paulmckenna.com/downloads

Go now to the website and use the password:

manifest123

and download the audio.

You must use both the written and the audio techniques in conjunction with each other to achieve optimum results. In particular, please listen to the hypnotic trance as often as you can to reinforce success.

Introduction

This book is about the closest thing to real magic you can get. When I was a child I watched the movies *Chitty Chitty Bang Bang* with flying cars and *Aladdin* with a genie appearing from a lamp to grant wishes. I also believed in Father Christmas. I thought if all I did was wish hard enough for something, then it would come true. However, life isn't like that ... or so I thought until my twenties when everything changed for me, because there is a way of using techniques that can help you get what you want. I'm going to share in this book my unique process to make your dreams come true, which I have developed over the past 40 years. It's different from ordinary manifesting. I call it Power Manifesting.

Power Manifesting is the act of creating something, and that can be from a single dream to transforming an entire life. In the three hours it takes to read this book and the hour you'll need to harness the psychological techniques, you will be able to Power Manifest what you truly want. Think of it this way – if there was a formula for success, would you be interested? This is not a glib soundbite.

I've created a series of techniques that are scientifically proven, in many cases, to work for most people most of the time. So if you do this, and follow the instructions to the letter, your life will get immeasurably better. Think of it as being like a set of algorithms that unlock your dreams and the life you truly want. Whether it's a car you've always aspired to, finding love, more money or to optimise your health, the tools you need to change things for the better are now in your hands. I say this with absolute certainty, as I have used these techniques myself, as have many super-achievers that I have studied.

The main reason I've written this guide is because one of my closest friends, the life coach to the stars Michael Neill, recently said to me: 'Paul, you get most of the things that you want. It's time to come out of the closet and admit you've manifested it.' Michael's words struck me as true. I struggled with dyslexia at school. One teacher told me I'd never amount to anything. I was also in the red at the bank when I first started manifesting. Yet, I've gone on to work with some of the world's most elite performers, athletes, entrepreneurs and even royalty. I have reinvented my career five times (radio DJ, stage hypnotist, TV broadcaster, self-help author, hypnotherapist). I've also found the love of my life after heartbreak and found fulfilment

INTRODUCTION

and purpose through my self-help and development books and courses.

Some people may think: 'Oh it's all right for you, you are rich.' I started with nothing. Nobody gave me any handouts, I borrowed money to pursue my dreams and I built everything myself. I've nearly lost it TWICE because I made some bad decisions along the way but I made every penny back. And if I can do it, you can do it. Each time I manifested a dream I set my sights higher. I have an amazing life through manifesting. But I have developed a super-powered, scientific approach to getting what you want. So, if you are not already manifesting a wonderful life for yourself then this book is for you. Even if you are already doing it, this will take it to another level. But don't take my word for it, put it to the test and see what happens.

This book and the accompanying audio techniques are like a personal coaching session with me. While you are reading it, don't be too surprised if you begin to notice you start to feel more clarity, optimism and motivation about your future. Each of the techniques are the keys that unlock Power Manifesting and, as you do them, the thought experiments and psychological techniques contained within this book will positively change the course of your life, in ways you hadn't dreamed possible before.

There are a number of techniques in this book that you can do yourself or, if you download the audio, I will walk you through each step. You will be doing an incredibly powerful psycho-sensory technique called Havening three times during the course of this process. This is because you have bought this guide for a result. Havening is part of a new field of therapy called 'psycho-sensory' that gives extraordinary results, fast. In just a few minutes we can reduce the emotional intensity of a feeling and establish calm, and it's been proven it also resets the brain. This book is about getting the life you want and this is the most powerful block remover I know. It forms a key part of a process that is like everything that I would do with you in a one-on-one manifesting session with me in print and audio. If you want to manifest the life you want, you need to allow yourself the time to do this. We are talking about a few hours of your life to read or listen to this book and a few minutes to do the techniques. You are about to plan the rest of your life, so please take time to do the techniques.

The difference that makes the difference

Around 20 years ago I wrote a book on confidence and recently I was interviewed by a radio broadcaster who'd read it at the time and practised the techniques in it. He liked a girl he worked alongside, and wanted to ask her on a date, but lacked the confidence. After he'd read the book, he decided to ask her out. I queried what happened and he said, 'We've been married for 15 years.'

Throughout this book are stories of people from science, entertainment, sport and business who have also manifested success in their life, which demonstrate again and again how one small change in yourself can create an exponential change in your entire life. So, as you read this book and do the techniques, you will start to notice how much better your life is becoming. Even though the techniques are very straightforward, you can also use the audio downloads where I guide you through each of them, just as I would if we were together one-to-one.

This book contains three sections to show you how to Power Manifest:

> 1. The first will get you clear about what you truly want and prime you so you can Power Manifest effectively.
>
> 2. The second section shows you step by step how to Power Manifest your dreams.
>
> 3. Section Three is a bonus chapter, which focuses on Advanced Power Manifesting, and it will give you the option to focus on five key areas of your life – **health, relationships and love, money, career** and **lifestyle and happiness** – in order to take things into quantum success.

This book uses Neuro-Linguistic Programming (NLP), which is a way of changing thoughts and behaviours in order to influence an outcome. You will suddenly be able to control your neuro-coding and harness your thoughts,

INTRODUCTION

feelings and behaviours, which will dramatically influence the results you get in the world. You will also harness the superpower of your internal timeline to manifest extraordinary changes in your life. Your internal timeline is the process by which pictures, movies and sounds of things that have happened to us, or events we know are going to happen, are positioned in our internal world. Our neuro-coding also records the past and present and plots the future. Power Manifesting gets you to notice and map where your mind KNOWS something is going to happen or something is true (like an event next week or how much money you have in the bank). You can then place something you WANT to happen (e.g. a successful business venture, a relationship or a bigger amount of cash flowing in your bank account) into that same place. This turbocharges all of your beliefs, focus, energy, thinking, motivation and actions to get that to happen. Most manifestors traditionally use vision boards and write down goals, which is 2D or 3D (where they include visualising), but this process takes it to 4D as you visualise and feel your dream within a timeline of your life.

If at this stage you may feel a little sceptical, that's OK. I don't expect you to believe me yet. In fact, I'd like you to try to prove me wrong. However, if you properly follow my techniques, which take just a few minutes each, it will be impossible for you not to have a significantly better and even more amazing life. Each time you do them you will get more from it, so you can repeat the exercises as often as you wish for a more powerful effect. I will share with you some of the most remarkable elements of my story along the way to help you understand how I have had such an extraordinary life and how I created it, so you will be able to, as well.

The hypnotic trance that accompanies this book will help you programme your unconscious mind to make you even more focused and relentless as you Power Manifest. It is as essential as the book itself, so you need to listen to it as often as you can. There is also a journal at the back of the book to keep you on track and help you monitor your progress.

One thing I'd urge you to do is not set the bar too low. Dream BIG! In fact, dream bigger than you ever thought possible before. It only takes a short amount of time to read this book, do the techniques and listen to the trance, so what do you have to lose? You have the power to be the architect of your life and destiny. So it's really a no-brainer.

INTRODUCTION

Using this system doesn't mean that you always get everything you want, when you want and suddenly everything is perfect. There will always be problems and challenges in everybody's life – that's how you learn and grow – but Power Manifesting will give you the tools to navigate your way through life with greater certainty and motivation. So, as you start to do this, if at any point you get Imposter Syndrome and think, 'I don't deserve this' or 'What if I get found out?' or 'Why me?', all that means is you've shifted up a gear, moved out of the zone of what you used to believe about yourself in terms of ability or success, and you've moved up the ladder of life. Just keep going and follow the process.

So now it's time to begin to realise your dreams. By the time you reach the end of Section Two, unstoppable change will already be underway. It's then your decision if you want to learn my Advanced Power Manifesting system. Either way, it's going to be amazing. And remember, if I can change my life, then so can you too. So let's get started.

Your baseline

If you think you can't Power Manifest, you'd be wrong. This is because everyone is a creative person. People have the misconception that only those who wear bow ties and work in ad agencies are creative types. But if you drive a car you create a journey, if you talk to someone you create a conversation, if you cook a meal you create a culinary experience. Look around you right now. Pretty much everything you see once started as an idea in someone's mind. From art and architecture to science, technology, even our gardens, it all started out as a dream. Some people are just better at creating their own life as they dream big and they make grand plans. Now you are going to be able to do that too.

So first, let's find out where you are right now. We can do this by looking at the foundations of a great life: **health**, **relationships and love**, **money**, **career** and **lifestyle and happiness**. I want you to mark, on a scale of one to ten, how you feel about each one right now. This gives us your baseline. I guarantee by the time you finish this book and after you've done all the exercises and listened to the hypnotic trance, your numbers will have dramatically changed for the better.

INTRODUCTION

- On a scale from 1 to 10, how would you rate your **health**, mental and physical? 6

- On a scale from 1 to 10, how would you rate your **relationships** (personal and professional) and **love**? 1

- On a scale from 1 to 10, how would you rate your **finances**? 6

- On a scale from 1 to 10, how would you rate your **career**? 6

- On a scale from 1 to 10, how would you rate your **lifestyle and happiness**? 3

Section One

The Foundations of Power Manifesting

Before I decided to write this book, I was concerned that some people might think Power Manifesting is some sort of 'woo woo', paranormal nonsense. This is because how manifesting works is still shrouded in some mystery.

Some people say it comes down to psychology and the focus of attention, and the triggering of a specific part of the brain that filters what is possible. Others argue that everything is already there in potential and it is simply down to the snowplough of perception that clears away everything that isn't what we need. Another hypothesis, again rooted in psychology, is that we are naturally inclined to spend more time working on what really matters to us and so that makes it more likely to happen. Mystics describe it as the oneness of energy and, because everything is energy, we just need to harness it. Many believe manifesting and its roots lie in spirituality. Another theory is based in science and that it aligns with quantum physics as energy affects energy. But there are other schools of thought too.

What is irrefutable is that there is a mountain of evidence that manifesting exists and works. I'm not arguing for an explanation or hypothesis in this book. Instead I'll signpost you to what's out there, and you can decide for yourself. So while at first glance, this seems to be a departure from my previous books, in reality, it's not. My self-help guides offer a solution or aspiration. This is what these pages contain.

The first step is to use a powerful psychological process to clear the way for you to Power Manifest. This is because it's an 'inside/out' job. While we cannot control everything that happens to us, we have a big say in how we think and what we do and this affects the results we get in the world.

Think of this point in your manifesting journey as boarding the best plane flight ever. You are waiting to take off, but you need to know where your destination is. When you Power Manifest, your plane flies on autopilot as both you and the universe are working in harmony towards your chosen destination. You may get blown slightly off course by strong winds, or unforeseen events, but you'll always know where you are going. Yet, most people spend more time making a list for the supermarket than they do planning the next year or five years of their life. So it's no wonder they never get to where they want to be as they didn't plan or work out how to execute it! The scientific evidence irrefutably shows people with a clearly defined vision are just way more likely to achieve it. This is opposed to wishing and hoping, which is why an estimated 80 per cent of New Year's Resolutions fail by 12 January. So let's set your vision and get clarity on it, so you can create the life you want.

How it works

We are going to use NLP and psycho-sensory techniques, which are cutting-edge psychological technologies that produce amazing results.

If you had a mobile phone in the Eighties it was the size of a brick and all you could do was make calls on it. Now phones are supercomputers and you can run your life in the palm of your hand. In the same way, psychological technology has made a massive leap in the last 20 years. It used to take psychiatrists months to cure a phobia or a trauma using systematic desensitisation or old traditional therapy. Now most are cured in minutes using NLP, which can identify and change behavioural patterns and heal trauma. A super-powerful NLP healing process will help you connect with your younger self and remove any conscious or unconscious blocks to Power Manifest what you want in life. This helps us because formative experiences early in life, or experiences that hurt us in some way later in life, can shape our beliefs, hold us back and stop us moving forward.

THE FOUNDATIONS OF POWER MANIFESTING

As any unconscious blocks are cleared away, then a series of techniques will get you to step into a new, empowered you. In order to manifest you also need to be clear about what you want so I'm going to take you through a self-insight process called 'Clean and Clear'. This is an inner feedback mechanism that gives you beautiful clarity about what you want in life. It will help you to visualise your dreams through a filter of what you are prepared to do (or not do) to attain them. This helps us to adapt so we can drop unrealistic expectations (e.g. 'I'll be a millionaire overnight') as well as barriers (e.g. 'I can't do this because...' or 'What if...?'). It means we can quickly abandon things that just won't pan out, and focus on those that can.

Being Clean and Clear is also vital because in order to manifest it has to be something you truly want, with no negative internal or external blocks, such as fear, self-sabotage or unnecessary doubt. I will also get you to dial up the extraordinary power of your emotional frequency and help you access your inner superpower of authenticity, both of which make manifesting even more likely to happen!

So are you ready? Then let's get started!

BUSINESS MANIFESTOR

Self-made billionaire Oprah Winfrey has said: 'I am a powerful manifestor. The way you think creates reality for yourself.' She manifested a role for herself in the 1985 movie *The Color Purple* by visualising it – and got an Oscar nomination.

Energy affects energy

I have already explained that there are many different schools of thought about how manifesting works. But a fundamental part of it is that energy affects energy. This is rooted in both science and spirituality. In her book *Manifest*, Roxie Nafousi states one of the most fundamental laws of manifesting;

Become the energy you want to attract.

One theory is that our thoughts and energy are connected with the outcome we get. In the realm of science we know that everything is atoms and molecules vibrating at a certain density and frequency. A quote that is sometimes attributed to Albert Einstein sums this up: 'Everything is energy and that's all there is to it. Match the frequency of the energy to the reality you want, and you cannot help but get that reality.' Quantum mechanics, which explains how the universe works on its smallest scales (and specifically quantum entanglement) has been used to describe, through the language of science, how manifesting relates to this constant flow of energy. Quantum entanglement suggests that when two particles link together in a certain way, no matter how far apart they are, they remain connected. The physicist and quantum visionary David Bohm theorised that every part of existence is interconnected, and we shape what is around us. He said: 'Thought creates the world.'

An extraordinary example of this in action happened with Dr Manjit Pope, a rocket scientist who used my techniques to manifest the birth of her son against seemingly insurmountable odds. Dr Pope was widowed in a car crash and due to the severity of her injuries four IVF clinics gave her just a 3 per cent chance of conceiving. She decided that even in medicine and against the odds doctors have been surprised by outcomes. She thought, 'I am going to be one of these miracles that surprise doctors!' And so she decided to manifest a baby. So she bought a doll from Toys R Us, wrapped it in a beautiful blanket and every night she would take it to bed, hold it in her arms and visualise already being a mother, as if it had happened. Her visualisation included hearing the baby, seeing herself as a mum cradling her child, and she added feelings (or frequency) by visualising how happy she would feel as she held her child. She told me: 'I thought people aren't going to believe a level-headed rocket scientist is doing manifestation.'

Yet, something utterly extraordinary happened. She and her friend David, who had offered to help her fulfil her dream of becoming a mum using IVF, fell in love and are now married, and she conceived naturally before her second round of IVF. She had a perfect pregnancy, and a perfect birth of her son Daya, who is now ten. She told me: 'Manifesting is science in action.' As a scientist, Dr Pope knows we are all made of atoms. Atoms are energy. Energy can't be destroyed. It changes from one form to another. So when we visualise something we put energy into it – whether it's positive or negative. 'Energy has vibrations and it can change form,' she added. 'That's what I believe happened to me.'

And Dr Pope is not alone in creating a physical touchstone (in her case a doll) to represent a dream she wanted to manifest. Another friend of mine fell in love with a blue, top-of-the-range, performance Lexus hybrid car. At the time he couldn't afford it on his salary, and it was more than double what he'd ever spent on a car before, so he manifested earning extra cash to purchase it. He got his son to create his touchstone by getting him to draw a picture of the car, which he then divided into 13 chunks. He told his little boy: 'Each time I'm able to put £5,000 towards the car, you can colour in one of the sections. When the car is completely coloured in, we are going to take your picture to the dealer and trade it for a real one?' His son thought it was the most exciting thing in the world. It took seven months for him to get it, when it should have taken him three years.

In the realm of spirituality there is clear evidence that energy affects energy. There was a remarkable study done by Randolph Byrd, who in the Eighties studied the effect of prayer (which is also another way of describing frequency and energy) on heart patients in a coronary care unit. Over ten months, 393 patients were split into two groups – one had people praying for them and the other did not. Those who had been prayed for had better outcomes and fewer complications!

Whether you support science, spirituality or both, one thing that is irrefutable is that our energy affects others. A friend of mine who owns a casino told me when someone is on too much of a winning streak, some venues stand somebody next to them called a 'cooler'. This is an extraordinarily unlucky person who just by being near to a winner changes their luck! There was a film about this phenomenon called *The Cooler* starring William H. Macy – but it's actually true! When I treat people with trauma using hypnotherapy, I also think in terms of my energy. I go to my happy, peaceful inner place first. I stay out of empathy but in compassion. This is because when you are empathetic with someone you feel their pain, which is obviously very unhelpful and it also depletes you. When you are compassionate, you stay in a strong place and are able to help them out of their pain. That way my energy can help them. In Chinese medicine things are described in terms of qi and flow, stagnation and life force, which are in the same family as 'energy'. Just as we can't put love under a microscope, but we know it exists, we can't put qi under a microscope, but we know energy or life force exists.

Another way that energy affects energy is when someone is angry or sad, you can sense it without the need to be told by them explicitly. A good example of this in action is a part of our physiology called 'mirror neurons', one of the most important discoveries of the past ten years in neuroscience. Mirror neurons are a collection of brain cells that respond when we see someone doing something by doing the same thing. So if someone genuinely smiles at you, you smile back at them as your brain is telling you to mirror them! It works negatively as well. It lets us understand feelings without words. So it's not a big step to consider that if you use Power Manifesting (harnessing the energy of the universe to get what you want) then that same energy can also help make dreams a reality.

So now I'm going to take you through a powerful two-step process to clear anything that may have been holding you back. You will then step into the new you, so you are primed and ready to Power Manifest. To do this we will ignite the power of both the conscious and unconscious mind. The conscious mind is the mind with which we actively and deliberately think all day long. You probably experience it as an internal voice that you think of as 'me'. But that is the 'smaller' mind as it can only hold a handful of ideas at any one time. The unconscious mind is the larger mind and our inner world. It is here that you store your memories, learning and habits and the automatic behaviours that you use every day to run your life. It regulates your biological functions including heartbeat and breathing, and contains your intelligence and wisdom. It is the source of your creativity.

Your mind is like a supercomputer. It files memories as pictures, movies and sounds in specific ways. This is neuro-coding. Pictures or movies that you are inside of and which are big, bold and bright have greater emotional intensity than ones that are dull and dim and where you are an external observer. *Where* the pictures and sounds are in your mind (near or far away, or to the left, centre or right) all have a significance and meaning. As you harness the power of your neuro-coding it's like having a secret superpower, as it influences your creativity, feelings and behaviours, gives you insights and ultimately affects the outcome you get in life.

Self-sabotage, self-doubt and having an Imposter Syndrome are three things that may block people from achieving their dreams. The first part of this process is the antidote to that. The second empowers you and takes the limiters off in order to open your mind to your massive potential. Rather than simply reading through this process, let me guide you through step by step with the audio that comes with this book. In addition, in the hypnotic trance that accompanies this book there is an energy booster to enhance and prime your mind and body too. Let's do it now.

STEP ONE:
HEALING THE YOUNGER YOU

🔊 Please read through this technique first, before you do it, or even better click on the audio and I will personally guide you through it.

1. Imagine a TV set over in the corner about 12 feet away from you.

2. On that TV set we are only going to see black and white movies.

3. Now, over there, allow a time to appear in black and white when you felt you needed reassurance.

4. Next, float over and into the screen, stop the world still and say 'hello' to the younger you.

5. Explain you are from the future and that you have come to help and heal the younger you.

THE FOUNDATIONS OF POWER MANIFESTING

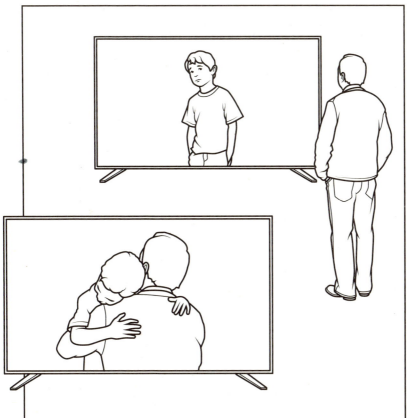

6   Tell the younger you what they need to hear to help and heal them and understand that they are OK.

7   When you have helped and healed the younger you, float out of the screen and back into yourself.

continued

POWER MANIFESTING

8   Now bring the younger you with you and place them in your heart and let the love in your heart help and heal them.

STEP TWO:
STEPPING INTO THE NEW YOU

🔊 Please read through this technique first, before you do it, or even better click on the audio and I will personally guide you through it.

Now we have healed the past, let's create a better future.

1. Close your eyes and imagine a cinema screen in front of you. On that screen see a you that is even healthier, happier and more successful. Notice your posture and the expression on your face, the light behind your eyes, the way you radiate joy. The sound of your voice is powerful and confident. Look at the way you gesture, and connect with others.

2. Next, imagine floating over and into the screen and step into that even more confident, healthier, happier and even more successful you. See through the eyes of your more confident, happier and more successful you. Hear your dialogue, which is strong and positive.

continued

POWER MANIFESTING

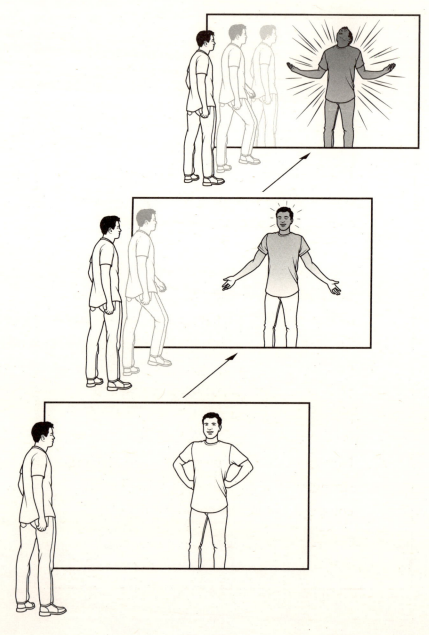

THE FOUNDATIONS OF POWER MANIFESTING

3   Now, imagine a cinema screen in front of you again. And on that screen see a you that is even healthier, happier and more successful. Notice your posture and the expression on your face. Notice the light behind your eyes. The sound of your voice is powerful and confident. Look at the way you gesture, and connect with others.

4   Next, imagine floating over and into yet another screen and step into that even more confident, healthier, happier and even more successful you. See through the eyes of your more confident, happier, successful you. Hear your dialogue, which is strong and positive.

5   Now notice where you feel the good feelings strongest of all in your body. Give them a colour (it can be any colour you like).

continued

6   Now, move that colour up through your neck into your head. Then move that colour all the way down through your shoulders into your arms and imagine moving it down through your chest into your legs and all the way to the tips of your toes.

7   Now, double the brightness, and double the intensity of the colour …

8   Feel the amazing feelings that go with it and imagine having this feeling for the rest of the day.

9   Feel this amazing feeling and imagine having this feeling for the rest of the week.

10 Feel this amazing feeling and imagine having this feeling for the rest of the month.

11 Feel this amazing feeling and imagine having this feeling in your home life.

12 Feel this amazing feeling and imagine having this feeling in your work life too.

My manifesting experience

Whenever I speak to a CEO, rock star, entrepreneur or super-achiever they always tell me they imagined, planned and then executed success. That is manifesting at work. It may surprise you, but I have Power Manifested this book that you are holding in your hands. When I create each of my self-help books I go off into the future and visualise flicking through each page, and I imagine and visualise as many details as I can in my mind's eye. At first it's just a sense of the tone of the book as I flick through the pages. Next, I start to get flashes of ideas of techniques or elements of structure. Eventually, I visualise holding the finished book (often months before publication) and I can see it clearly, hear the tone and notice how it makes me feel. I do this until I get a feeling of the tone of it and repeat this process at key stages during its development. In the first week I started writing, synchronicities started happening. Time after time, people kept asking me: 'Do you know anything about manifesting?' It was like the universe was listening and directing me to put pen to paper!

A series of extraordinary events led me to start manifesting. Prior to becoming a hypnotherapist and life coach, in the Eighties I worked as a DJ for Capital Radio, but I felt something was missing and I hadn't reached my full potential. My life changed when a friend suggested I try manifesting. One of my friends at the station said that he used this strange technique to manifest parking spaces: when he visualised them, usually within a few minutes he'd find a parking spot in central London.

One night on my way to rehearse for my first ever hypnotic show at the Duke of York's Theatre in London after I'd borrowed a year's wages from the bank – so a massive amount was at stake – I couldn't park. As I went up and down the streets there wasn't a single space in the heart of theatreland. I'd given a lift to my friend and he said: 'I always ask the parking fairies to find me a space. Why don't you try it?' I thought it was bonkers and the nuttiest thing ever, so I thought: 'I'll prove you wrong.' I said: 'Please find me a parking space!' Lo and behold, within moments I found a spot! To be honest, I think I had tuned my brain to find one by saying it out loud. But I kept doing it afterwards, and almost all of the time a parking space showed up pretty quickly. I thought there must be a scientific reason for this; maybe I was just more alert to spotting them.

The game changer for me was almost inexplicable, but I think of it as serendipity. As if by coincidence, a colleague of mine revealed he was manifesting his dream of becoming a travel journalist and flying on Concorde. He created a vision board featuring all these amazing places, including a beautiful village in Switzerland he'd seen in a magazine where he wanted to go. Every Sunday he packed his bags and he got the experience and excitement of packing to go on a trip. Similarly to Dr Pope's miracle son, or the purchase of the Lexus mentioned earlier, he used the first key to manifesting:

Act as if it had already happened. What do you see, hear and feel as you visualise it?

My friend would even go to Heathrow Airport and get in the queue, then he'd go home and watch a video (this was before streaming!) of what it was like to fly on Concorde and give himself a sensory-rich experience. Within weeks he was called into his boss's office and asked to do a special series of international travel reports around the world. One of his first assignments was actually flying on Concorde! He later got sent to Switzerland and he thought: 'This place looks familiar.' When he returned home he checked his vision board and it was the exact same village that he had been manifesting. When he told me this I thought: 'OK, I'm going to give this a go, too.'

At the time I was in the red with the bank and the first thing I manifested was financial freedom. I got my bank statement and I cut out the red 'overdrawn' number from it. I then glued a new number onto the paper. It said, '£77,000 in credit.' I burst out laughing because it felt a bit ridiculous and unattainable, but there I was looking at it and somehow it also felt strangely possible. I left it where I could see it, on my fridge door, and looked at it every day. I focused upon it and also imagined walking out to a full theatre, hearing the applause and feeling the feeling of success. I had no way of creating that sort of money, but a few weeks later the opportunity of doing a major run of my new hypnotic show became possible at the much larger Dominion Theatre. So suddenly a lot was at stake. After my initial six weeks, incredibly, despite turning over £50,000, we were left £300 in the red. It was as though the universe had conspired against me. An accountant friend of mine popped round and asked: 'Why are you looking so glum?' He told me: 'All you have to do is adapt what you are doing slightly and you will make money! You are closer to success than you realise.' So I decided I would do everything to manifest success on this new run. I took a photo of myself

THE FOUNDATIONS OF POWER MANIFESTING

outside the theatre next to the 'House Full' sign before it even started. I also pinned it on my fridge so I could see it all the time, and imagined what it would be like to play to a full house, over and over again. The first week we were about half full, not a comfortable feeling, but the next week we were three quarters full and by the third week the show was sold out! The new run turned into a triumph! It was a glorious feeling and one that I would experience again and again and teach others to attain as well.

Within a matter of months I was in credit beyond the £77,000 and I have been a serious manifestor ever since. Over the years I have honed my method and it has enabled me to live a life beyond my wildest dreams. Each time I'd Power Manifest something wonderful, I set my sights higher. My ultimate goal was to one day be able to help people through hypnotherapy and NLP – and I am now living that dream while doing a job that I love. People might say: 'Oh it's all right for you.' Of course success is just luck, ask any failure. However, actually I built everything I have for myself. I've had help because people were kind to me, but you will get that help too when you start to Power Manifest – as what you don't know is that, once you start down this path, help shows up. You may not have it when you start. Things may look impossible. But help comes just at the moment when you need it. And as you begin to manifest, your energy and frequency rise as you get the hang of it, and you find you are able to do it again and again. You begin to believe just how amazing things can be once you start – it's extraordinary!

Right now you should be starting to get curious about the power of manifesting. So let's learn the simple process of how it works before you go and do it.

HOLLYWOOD MANIFESTOR

Hollywood star Jim Carrey has said: 'I wrote myself a cheque for $10 million for acting services rendered and I set myself three years.' He found out he was going to make $10 million on *Dumb and Dumber* shortly before his deadline.

Raise your frequency

So now I want to introduce you to the idea of your emotional frequency and its role in Power Manifesting. Remember, one of the theories of manifesting is that we constantly emit a frequency based on our emotions, and in simple terms *we get back what we put out.* Your state of mind and body is key, as if you are not in a great place, such as angry or frightened, then you are transmitting on a low frequency. But if you are in a state of love, happiness, joy and creativity – all the good stuff – you are transmitting on a high frequency. And there is a simple scientific explanation for this ...

The Law of Sympathetic Resonance in music shows that one thing can physically affect another, even if they don't seem to be directly connected. If you have two pianos in the same room and you hit a C note on one of them, you will find that the C string on the other piano will start vibrating at the same rate. The frequency of someone who is angry is different to the frequency of someone who is happy. Misery loves company. And how is it that all the lucky, happy and rich people seem to find each other? It's all down to sympathetic resonance and frequency!

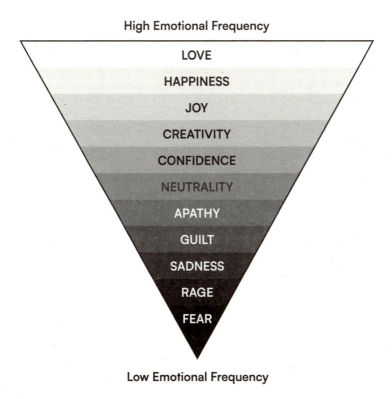

A 2007 study by the Korean National Institute of Agricultural Biotechnology also found that plants grow better when they are exposed to classical music. The vibrations (or frequency) of classical music are thought to act in a similar way to a massage on their molecular structure. The Royal Philharmonic Orchestra once released an album to help plants grow based on similar research. A lot of people talk to their plants for this reason too. So if you want to whisper sweet nothings to your sweet peas, science suggests there could be some benefit! And it's all down to frequency!

Energy and frequency, in rare cases, can also heal. For many years, I have worked with a renowned energy healer called Seka Nikolic who counts everyone from 'incurables' to royalty around the world as her clients. She always talks in terms of frequency when she's healing someone. My father Bill had severe rheumatoid arthritis and he was told by his doctor he was going to soon have to be in a wheelchair. It's fair to say he was very sceptical about alternative therapies, but my mother persuaded him to go and see her and the results were miraculous. After a week of healing from Seka he came round to see me and he looked years younger. The first words he said to me were: 'I'm healed!' When he later went for tests at his hospital, they couldn't find a trace of the arthritis in his body.

One day when we were working together, Seka said to me: 'I've noticed the frequency and energy of your words are healing when you speak, I see them as colours coming from your mouth.' I understand that to mean I am bathing people in sound when I hypnotise them.

So as you raise your frequency it's important to tap into the frequency of love, happiness, optimism and creativity as much of the time as possible. The more time you spend around people who lift your energy up – who are lucky, joyous and successful – the more likely it is that you are going to experience that too. So now it's time to optimise your frequency by using a deceptively simple NLP process to prime you further for Power Manifesting. This takes just a few minutes and I can take you through this process if you listen to the audio that comes with this guide too.

THE FREQUENCY BOOSTER

🔊 Please read through this technique first, before you do it, or even better click on the audio and I will personally guide you through it.

1. Close your eyes and imagine a cinema screen in front of you.

2. Now imagine you are looking at a version of you that has a higher frequency, a you that is in a state of joy, peace, gratitude, kindness and optimism.

3. Notice the expression on your face, your posture, the way you radiate happiness.

4. Now, imagine floating into the screen and step into your higher-frequency self.

5. See the world and life through your happier self. Hear your internal dialogue – kind, optimistic and reassuring – saying to yourself 'all is well' and feel how good this state of higher frequency feels.

6   Next, notice where in your body you feel the best feelings and give the feelings a colour.

7   Now imagine moving that colour up through your neck, into your head, down through your shoulders, arms and fingers. Move the colour down through your chest to your legs and then to the tips of your toes.

8   Now double the brightness and intensity of the colour and then double it again.

9   Now, imagine being surrounded by this colour and living in this higher frequency for the rest of the day.

10   Imagine being surrounded by this colour every day and living in this higher frequency in every part of your life going forward – in your health, relationships and love, money, career, and lifestyle and happiness.

The authenticity zone

Now you have boosted your energy and frequency, we're going to stack them together with a super-powerful state called the zone of authenticity. Authenticity means different things to different people but its definition is 'the quality of being real and true'. When you are in a state of authenticity, you are comfortable in your own skin, and you reinforce the feeling: 'I am enough'. Authenticity can also encompass passion and drive; it is something heartfelt and it flows. Being authentic (true to yourself and what you believe in) is important due to the fact some manifestors believe you attract what you *feel*. People can feel when someone is being authentic (as opposed to desperate or manipulative) so it's an incredibly powerful state to be in.

The extraordinary power of authenticity was revealed in a study using the SPANE (short for the Scale of Positive and Negative Experience) scale of emotion. This measures positive and negative energy. According to the biologist Gary Brecka, thousands of people agreed to take part in a study where researchers measured the frequency that was leaving their bodies. The results were astounding. They were able

THE FOUNDATIONS OF POWER MANIFESTING

to decipher people's frequencies in such detail they could tell what *mood* the volunteer was in. Gary says the most powerful frequency to leave a human's body is 'authenticity.' So your state of authenticity really is an inner superpower!

When we fear being disliked, believe we are not good enough or are desperate for love and approval, we are not our authentic selves. This technique is the antidote to that and it leaves you in a beautiful clean state of authenticity. It also uses a super-powerful form of NLP called Havening therapy, which was created by my friend Ronald Ruden MD. Ph.D. Scientific studies have shown that it is amazingly effective at relieving sadness and reducing stress, trauma and compulsion. But it also removes both conscious and unconscious obstacles. It is so powerful that we are going to use it in three different ways during the course of this book.

Dr Ruden's work has been hailed as a remarkable breakthrough. He discovered that patterns of repeated touch to parts of the body combined with specific eye movements and visualisations have a rapid, reliable and predictable effect on our feelings. The patterns of touch used in Havening are what enable a mother to comfort her baby and they are hardwired into every infant. Havening combines these deep-rooted patterns of reassurance and comfort with sequences to break down the associations that triggered unhappy feelings or created blocks. This technique is not merely a distraction. Numerous scientific studies have proven that the Havening technique reduces stress chemicals in our body and produces states of relaxation and calm. We also change the way our brain processes thoughts and feelings. So now let's get into the authenticity zone with this technique. Even though this will only take you a few minutes to do, if you want me to take you through this process step by step personally, go to the audio now.

THE FOUNDATIONS OF POWER MANIFESTING

GET INTO THE AUTHENTICITY ZONE

🔊 Please read through this technique first, before you do it, or even better click on the audio and I will personally guide you through it.

PART ONE

1. Close your eyes and summon any feelings of fear of being disliked, unworthiness or self-loathing.

2. Rate them on a scale of 1 to 10.

3. Put your right hand on your left shoulder and your left hand on your right shoulder.

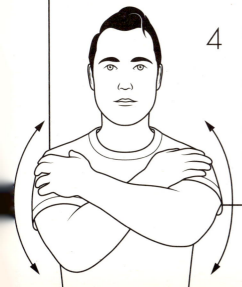

4. Begin gently stroking the sides of your arms from the top of your shoulder to your elbow. Continue to do this throughout this process.

continued

5   When the uncomfortable feelings are at their peak, clear your mind.

6   Now, imagine you are walking on a beach and with each footstep in the sand count out loud from 1 to 20.

7   Next, remember a time when you felt really happy and return to it again like you are back there again now. Make the colours rich and bold, the sounds loud and the feelings strong.

8   Notice where the feelings are strongest in your body and give them a colour.

9   Now imagine moving that colour up to the top of your head and down to the tips of your toes, so you are bathed in that colour.

10   Still stroking the sides of your arms, imagine walking in a garden and count out loud from 1 to 20 with each footstep you take.

11   Now stop and notice how much the uncomfortable feelings have reduced.

PART TWO

1   Close your eyes and summon any feelings of being desperate for love and approval.

2   Rate them on a scale of 1 to 10.

3   Put your right hand on your left shoulder and your left hand on your right shoulder.

4   Begin gently stroking the sides of your arms from the top of your shoulder to your elbow. Continue to do this throughout this process.

5   When the uncomfortable feelings are at their peak, clear your mind.

6   Now, imagine you are walking on a beach and with each footstep in the sand count out loud from 1 to 20.

continued

7 Next, remember a time when you felt really happy and return to it again like you are back there again now. Make the colours rich and bold, the sounds loud and the feelings strong.

8 Notice where the feelings are strongest in your body and give them a colour.

9 Now imagine moving that colour up to the top of your head and down to the tips of your toes, so you are bathed in that colour.

10 Still stroking the sides of your arms, imagine walking in a garden and count out loud from 1 to 20 with each footstep you take.

11 Now stop and notice how much the uncomfortable feelings have reduced.

Now you have optimised your frequency and energy and got into the zone of authenticity, you are ready to take the next step. It's time to get clarity on your dreams in an amazing thought process called 'Clean and Clear' because it's essential to have a clear vision of what you want to manifest.

Getting Clean and Clear

If you aren't clear about your dream, how are you going to get it? It's like setting off in a boat without a rudder – you can end up anywhere. This next process may require a little more concentration but give it your all, as it's for your future. So think of the time spent doing this as an investment in yourself, because gaining clarity requires a commitment and a decision to give time to reflect and assimilate.

To start with, I'd like you to connect with the *feeling* you need to tap into that indicates you are Clean and Clear. So, imagine you are hungry and you really want pizza for lunch! If you think: 'I fancy a pizza but I really shouldn't because I'll blow my diet', that is the feeling that says you *haven't* reached Clean and Clear yet. In contrast, getting the feeling: 'YES I want pizza!!' IS the feeling you are looking for. It's a 'no-brainer' feeling. And now you know what feeling you are looking to connect with, ask yourself this simple question:

What do you already know that you want?

Whether you realise it or not, you already know what you want, up to a point. So, it's time to choose five things you really want in your life. To start, I want you to do a practice run because this is a bit like going to the gym and using your muscles for the first time. So I recommend you start small with things like: 'I want a perfect cup of coffee in bed in the morning' or 'to catch up with a friend'. The purpose of this is to connect with that 'pizza' or no-brainer feeling. THEN you can move to bigger things, like picking up the keys to a new car, jetting off on your dream holiday or a perfect date night. Get creative and have fun with this and really embrace that feeling!

Once you are really familiar with that 'pizza' feeling, then you can choose five BIG dreams. These are the ones you are going to Power Manifest in Section Two. My five 'no-brainer dreams' are health, my happy marriage, fulfilment in my job, financial security, and having good times with wonderful friends. When I think of them I have got that 'pizza' feeling. They are 'no-brainers' for me. Your dreams may be different and that's OK!

In his book *The DNA of Success*, Jack Zufelt created a sliding scale from one to 100, which can help you to see if you have a no-brainer dream. At the bottom of his scale are wishes that are unrealistic. At the top of his scale are heartfelt, authentic dreams, which are driven by passion and energy – and these are the 'no-brainers'! While he calls it the Core Desire Scale, it can also be seen as a dream scale. Aim to get your dreams as close to 80 or above, if possible, because if you aren't fully invested in them they are less likely to happen.

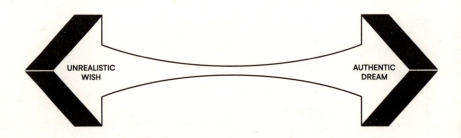

THE CORE DESIRE SCALE

- 1 to 20 are wishes that have little substance in reality.

- 20 to 40 are things you feel you should do due to external pressure rather than what you really want.

- 40 to 60 are dreams you'd quite like, but aren't fully invested in.

- 60 to 80 are recurring dreams you've considered on and off, and which are evolving and growing in your mind. Often they are connected with things you feel you *should* do.

- 80 to 99 are dreams you'd like to accomplish; they are important to you and they spark your passion.

- 100 is a truly authentic, heartfelt dream.

Ecology checks

Ecology is really just the study of consequences. It's really important to build pictures or movies of yourself looking happy and healthy into the vision of your future when you Power Manifest your dreams. So next I want you to ask yourself:

What are you prepared to do to get what you want?

What are you NOT prepared to do to get what you want?

Is there a cost to yourself or others in terms of health/mood/financial status?

Can you visualise yourself doing it?

It will be really helpful to write your answers down. For example, when I asked myself the first question in terms of love, I was ready to open my heart. When I asked myself the second question, I realised I didn't want to settle for second best as I wanted true love, and the third answer was that there was no cost to myself if it worked out! And I visualised myself with the love of my life, even down to their qualities and values and things we'd enjoy doing together. I got specific! So falling in love and marrying Kate really was a no-brainer for me!

I never forget asking one guy what he wanted and for his lifestyle he replied: 'A big house, a flash car and a boat.' When I then asked him, 'Where are you in this picture?', he replied: 'I didn't think about me.' I told him: 'So you are going to work yourself to death to get all of this, are you?' Whenever you're visualising or manifesting, make sure you include yourself in this vision looking healthy, happy and successful.

BUSINESS MANIFESTOR

Billionaire and Spanx founder Sara Blakely was given a self-help tape by her dad as a teen. She has said: 'It was talking about visualisation, the Law of Attraction, not caring what other people think about you, not being consumed by the fear of failure ... and the clouds parted for me.'

Removing blocks

If you get to this point and you still feel stuck, and there's not an obvious reason why, it may be because a part of you thinks you don't deserve it, you think you won't be able to handle it, or maybe you suffer from Imposter Syndrome. This next process will remove any unnecessary blocks. This uses a second version of the super-powerful method of Havening, which has been hailed, by so many eminent people, as one of the greatest breakthroughs in modern therapy. Numerous scientific studies have shown the effect of the specific sequence of Havening that I will now share with you, which resets the way that your brain interprets and responds to blocks. This actually alters the pathways in your brain.

During this process you will connect with your unconscious mind and ask it to show you the block. The unconscious mind will offer an abstract symbol which represents it. For some it's a brick wall, or even a dark pile of sludge – your unconscious mind will tell you. As you concentrate on the block and then do the Havening technique, it will either immediately disappear or do so incrementally. Afterwards, people suddenly find that area of their life dramatically improves. You can also use this technique if your core desires are at 60 or 70 per cent, to free any unconscious blocks around them too. I recommend everyone do it at least once as it's liberating and empowering.

THE BLOCK REMOVER

🔊 Please read through this technique first, before you do it, or even better click on the audio and I will personally guide you through it.

1. Close your eyes and summon anything that is blocking you from achieving what you want.

2. Rate the block on a scale of 1 to 10.

3. Put your right hand on your left shoulder and your left hand on your right shoulder.

4. Begin gently stroking the sides of your arms from the top of your shoulder to your elbow. Continue to do this throughout this process.

5. When the uncomfortable block feelings are at their peak, clear your mind.

6. Now, imagine you are walking on a beach and with each footstep in the sand count out loud from 1 to 20.

7. Next, remember a time when you felt really happy and return to it again like you are back there again now. Make the colours rich and bold, the sounds loud and the feelings strong.

8. Notice where the feelings are strongest in your body and give them a colour.

9. Now imagine moving that colour up to the top of your head and down to the tips of your toes, so you are bathed in that colour.

10. Still stroking the sides of your arms, imagine walking in a garden and count out loud from 1 to 20 with each footstep you take.

continued

> 11 Now stop and notice what has happened to the block and how much it has reduced.
>
> 12 If it has gone, that is excellent. If, however, there's still a little of the block there, just repeat the process until it's gone or almost gone, leaving you free to manifest what you want.

A friend of mine did this process in order to manifest true love while she was waiting for a flight. When she visualised herself with him, he turned up almost exactly as she'd manifested him – even down to him putting the loo seat down! They are also happily married!

Just a few words of caution. You are not looking for perfection. You should look for someone you can be your true, authentic self with. Also be specific if you are looking for love, as many people meet their EX partner this way, as they forget to put in their list that key ingredient!

Now I want you to write your five dreams down. You can do this in stages if you wish. You can even choose one dream to move forward with and choose the rest of your dreams later.

YOUR FIVE DREAMS

1.

2.

3.

4.

5.

Over the years, several times I have reached Clean and Clear, done my ecology checks, removed any unconscious blocks ... and then there will be a moment of serendipity, where the universe seemingly conspires in my favour. Often there will be an unexpected email or a phone call that sets it in motion.

This happened very recently to a friend of mine who used my Power Manifesting method to attract some new business. He thought: 'It's been a few months since I worked with a global entrepreneur.' So he sat down and Power Manifested working with one. Just one day later, his PA rang him and said: 'Do you know this billionaire? He's just reached out to you.' Then the next day she rang again and said: 'Do you know this huge Italian pop star? He just DM'd you.' Both of them hired him!

The philosopher Henry David Thoreau once said: 'If one advances confidently in the direction of his dreams and endeavours to live the life which he has imagined, he will meet with a success unexpected in common hours.' And that's Power Manifesting in action!

Congratulations! You have completed the first stage of Power Manifesting by getting your Clean and Clear dreams you want to manifest. In Section Two we are going to tap into focus, intuition, luck and momentum. Then we are going to harness the power of your internal timeline to set your Power Manifesting into motion! It's an exciting prospect, isn't it?

Section Two

Power Manifesting in Action

By this point, not only will you have clarity about what you want but you will be feeling a real sense of positivity as your frequency and authenticity has been optimised. Now, in Section Two the BIG stuff is coming as you are going to Power Manifest your dreams and set them in motion. So let's get started.

SPORTING MANIFESTOR

The most decorated Olympian Michael Phelps mentally rehearses his swimming races. He has said: 'I would visualise probably a month or so in advance just of what could happen, what I want to happen and what I don't want to happen – because when it happened I was prepared for it.'

How it works

You are going to significantly increase your **focus, decision-making, luck** and **intuition** in this section. You will also harness the power of **action** and **momentum** as Power Manifesting needs ACTION to make it happen. When you stack these together and direct them at something you want, firstly you program your unconscious mind and tell it 'make all of my thoughts, behaviours and direction in life, focus like a laser beam to make it happen'. Then, in the finale of this section, I will show you how to set the dreams you want to Power Manifest in motion using your internal timeline. Placing something you *want* to happen on your internal timeline tells the brain to act like a heat-seeking missile and it directs all of your thoughts, feeling, behaviours and energy to propel you where you want to go even faster and more efficiently! Your mind will be relentless in propelling you towards your target!

The power of Five Minutes of Focus

I'm often asked: 'What's the one piece of advice you would give people?' The answer is simple:

You get more of what you focus on in life.

What you think, you become. Far too many people spend too much time thinking about what they *don't* want (such as 'I don't want to be single, shy or overweight') – and they make it a self-fulfilling prophecy. In other words, they manifest it. The co-creator of NLP Dr Richard Bandler has a great saying: 'Disappointment requires adequate planning.' In other words, thinking too much about what you don't want is more likely to make it happen. Now it's time to focus on what you DO want! So, even though you want to consider things that could go wrong, so they can be headed off at the pass, you need to put more energy into what you **WANT** to happen.

Self-made legendary investor and philanthropist Warren Buffett, whose fortune is an estimated $130 billion, was once asked: 'What is the secret of your success?' He reportedly said: 'Focus.' Yet we live in a world where people are losing their ability to focus. Professor Gloria Mark, a psychologist at the University of California, Irvine and author of *Attention Span*, has found over two decades that our ability to focus has been in decline. Back in 2004 the average attention span on a screen was two and a half minutes. But in recent years, she has found, it has plummeted to just 47 seconds on average. Conversely, numerous studies have found that if you can find something you are genuinely interested in, then your concentration level will soar. So improving your focus can give you an edge and help you to realise your new future.

Changing your life can take the amount of time it takes to brush your teeth. Just five minutes of focus is said to have made Andrew Carnegie, a 19th-century Scottish-born industrialist, one of the richest men in the world in his day. He made his fortune in America and the story goes that he faced an investigation on behalf of Congress, who thought he must have sharp business practices to be as wildly successful as he was. Yet investigators could find no evidence of wrongdoing. So they asked him how he amassed such mind-boggling wealth – the equivalent of an estimated $310 BILLION today. He is said to have told them it was all down to five minutes of pure focus.

So now we're going to train your brain, one step at a time, to eventually focus for five minutes at a time. This process takes practice, so allow yourself to learn it like any skill – one step at a time. I want you to focus on your dream and think about what you can do to get there. Set a timer, and FOCUS! Stop the timer when your brain wanders or you get to 30 seconds. That gives you a start point. Repeat again until you get to one minute, then two minutes, then three minutes, followed by four minutes, until you get to five minutes over the course of a day. When you get to five minutes or close to it you are in a different league to other human beings on the planet. That means you are different – you have a superpower!

Dr Richard Bandler was one of a number of experts who did a similar, incremental process with the US military to improve their sharp-shooting skills. At the time the army was giving its soldiers weapons and asking them to start shooting at 100 yards away, and concluding that some people were just poor shots. So he changed the model and started everyone at 10 yards. They were then moved back from the target in stages of 20 yards, 30 yards, and so on. Their shooting scores went through the roof. It meant everyone was able to hit the target as everyone was set up for success. It's a simple process called chunking; if you break a task down into small enough chunks, almost anything is possible.

An extreme example, which demonstrates this point at the other end of the spectrum, is the extraordinary Michel Lotito, known as Monsieur Mangetout, who once ate an entire Cessna 150 aeroplane. He broke it down into chunks and did it over the course of two years. Nonetheless he did it! One lady lost ten stone using my weight loss system and she went on to run three marathons. I asked her: 'How did you start running?' She started by walking her dog. Then she decided to walk slightly further each day. Eventually she decided to try the NHS Couch To 5K App and ran for one minute on and one minute off at first. Then, a few months later, she went for a half marathon before going on to run full marathons. Just like the American shooters and the plane eater, she reached her goal in increments.

So, every day, I'd like you to repeat this Five Minutes of Focus exercise, to focus for just a little bit longer and longer each day. That's all it takes. Your aim, long term, is to do five minutes straight. Just like an Olympian who is going for gold, it takes incremental practice and improvement over time, sometimes two steps forward and one back, but always moving in the direction of success.

As you start to build your focus, you will get a feeling of subtle power. Eventually when you get to five minutes of focus you will notice there is a profound change in your feelings and perception. That's the game changer! Remember, while you're aiming for five minutes, it's OK if you don't get there straightaway. Any focus is better than no focus at all! However, you can also incrementally increase your focus over the course of a few days or even weeks, to add up to five minutes in total. In the journal at the back of this guide is a space to write how long you've been able to concentrate for, so you can monitor your progress. This will help you to track your progress because scientific research shows us an important rule:

What gets measured, gets done!

My manifesting experience

I once went to a big event at the Grosvenor House Hotel where my friend Simon Cowell was being honoured for his contribution to the music industry. He is an absolute juggernaut, not just as a TV personality but in terms of acts that he's discovered. We were sitting and watching as one superstar after another got up and said: 'I owe my career to Simon.' I remember turning to him and saying: 'Did you ever think that something like this would happen?' And he said: 'Yes, actually I did. I imagined one day this would happen to me.' We both laughed ... but Simon is a man with extraordinary focus, vision, clarity and great instincts. He listens to his gut, he has made his own luck, made great decisions and taken action and, even though he wouldn't call it this, I have learned a lot from him about what I call manifesting in action.

I've already told you that when I first started manifesting, I used scissors to cut out the overdrawn figure on my bank statement and put in its place a big bank balance, along with manifesting my theatre success. But when I think back, I have actually fulfilled another early dream with manifesting. Along with *Chitty Chitty Bang Bang* and *Aladdin*, as a 16-year-old I loved the movie *10* with Dudley Moore. I remember thinking his character's lifestyle was the pinnacle of success. As I sat in the cinema 40-odd years ago, I thought: 'I want that.' In the movie Dudley lived in a beautiful house in the Hollywood Hills, he had a convertible Rolls-Royce and a swimming pool and all the cool people hung out with him. Simon Cowell and I were chatting one day and I said to him: 'Have you ever watched the movie *10*?' And he said, 'Yes.' I laughed as I said to him, 'As a kid I really wanted to be Dudley Moore.' Simon told me: 'I think you might have turned into him!'

As I started purposefully manifesting, I manifested success for myself over and over again. For instance, I manifested myself having a successful show on American TV. I sat down every day and I visualised making the TV show. I would look at a TV set and imagine turning it on and seeing myself on it, the audience figures being great, and every detail of the show as if it was already happening. Within a year it happened.

I have also told you that I manifested my soulmate Kate bringing love into my life. It's been reported that I used an Excel spreadsheet to find Kate. That is not true as I don't even know how to use Excel! But I definitely did manifest love. It is true that my brain drew a spreadsheet of my dream partner and at the top was Kate, who had been a part of my team for decades. That's when I realised that the woman I'd been looking for all my life was already in it. At first I was gutted at two and a half decades of missed time together. I spoke to an astrologer friend of mine just after we began dating and I confided that I felt sad that we'd lost the potential of so many years together, but he said: 'Paul, it would never have worked out before – it was all about timing. You both had to come to this point in your lives to be where you are now for love to happen.'

How one good decision can change your life

Now you are training your brain to focus, the next step is to harness it to make better decisions. Your decisions have got you to where you are right now. It's important to take responsibility for that and for yourself. So first, you will need to consciously step out of any 'victim mindset' you might have and into an 'owner mindset' so you become the architect of your own destiny. It is important to emphasise here that this does not refer to you as a victim in terms of your identity. This concerns purely your attitude – which shapes your actions and ultimately the outcome you get. Anyone who has a 'victim mindset' is powerless. When people are thinking and behaving as a victim they are simply reacting. However, if you change your attitude, and take ownership of your life, you become proactive. This is known as having an 'owner mindset'. Otherwise you are a victim of circumstance. So let's harness the owner mindset now!

My friend Steve Crabb, the Quantum Growth Coach, has a great way to shift you out of a victim mindset and into an owner mindset. One day we did this simple process together to work out if I had a victim mindset or an owner mindset in business and love. I remember him saying to me, 'So you've had some bad things happen early on in your business?' I said, 'Yes, someone stole from me and things didn't work, but it was my choice to go into that project.' He immediately said, 'Then you have an "owner mindset".' He then said (and this was prior to meeting Kate): 'Let's talk about relationships.' I admitted: 'I'm in a cycle of dating the same type of woman and breaking up and then doing it all again.' He said, 'So it's all about them, is it?' I said, 'Yes!' He pointed out: 'There's a common denominator here and it's YOU! So you are thinking and behaving as a victim!'

When I took responsibility and recognised that I had a part to play in what happened, I restored my power. As I took responsibility, I could take charge and change things for the better. My friend's question was one of several events that made me aware of what I was doing, and that awareness was the first step towards changing it. So take the time to interrogate yourself. Going forward, try to consciously take ownership of your decisions. It is hugely empowering as it means you are proactive and in the driving seat of your own life. That transformed how I approached relationships and now I have been happily married for eight years!

Upside/Downside

Now we have looked at making proactive decisions, it's time to learn how we can make great decisions more consistently. There is rarely 100 per cent certainty in any decision-making process and a well-known saying is: 'Risk is the currency of the gods.' A key part of any good decision strategy is analysing and mitigating risk. The Body Shop founder, the late Anita Roddick, once told me: 'I've never met a super-successful person who takes risks. They take educated, calculated risks.'

The billionaire Richard Branson has a great technique for this, which I'm going to share with you now. He uses a strategy called 'Upside/Downside.' The principle is that with any objective you ask yourself two questions. Firstly, 'What's the upside to this?' Secondly, 'What's the downside?' If the downside is too high and the upside is too low, don't do it. If something has a very high upside and a low downside then TAKE MASSIVE ACTION!

So let's say you'd like to launch a business, but you decide to keep working while you launch it. The upside is you could get some extra income and if it takes off you can jack in the day job. The downside is you will have longer working hours and you will need to put up some money to get things started. So the upside is an eight. The downside is a four (as you could lose some cash if it goes wrong) – but only if you can afford to lose that amount of money. On the other hand, if you worked out that you couldn't afford to lose any cash as you could end up losing your home, then the upside and downside would change. In these circumstances the upside would be an eight and the downside would be a ten. Then the smarter decision would be to look for a lower-risk opportunity, more suited to your current circumstances. This can apply to any aspect of your life. For instance, in dating and relationships if there's somebody you want to ask out, if you really like them and are single the downside may be a three – you will feel bad for a few hours or a day or two if you are rejected. But the upside is they may say yes and you end up having a fantastic relationship, so it's a ten!

I was recently offered a big business opportunity, and if things all went according to plan the upside was a ten. But there was an element of risk that meant if it went wrong I stood to lose a lot of money. That meant it had a downside of ten too. I didn't do it. The downside must always be low and the upside very high.

Never do anything on a 50/50. There has got to be a huge upside and low downside in order for you to take action. A friend of mine who is a billionaire hotelier recently told me about a great example of Upside/Downside in action. He paid an eye-watering sum for a hotel and its wonderful golf course, despite the fact the building itself was run down. However, he figured out that the land alone was worth the millions he paid. So even if he bulldozed the entire thing he would get his money – and more – back. So he bought it because the upside was massive, and the downside was very low. Once again, it's a deceptively simple technique where the difference makes all the difference.

HOLLYWOOD MANIFESTOR

Hollywood actor and martial artist Bruce Lee wrote himself a mission statement: 'I, Bruce Lee, will be the first highest paid Oriental superstar in the United States.' I've seen it. You could see the determination in his handwriting and almost feel the energy coming off it!

Make five good decisions in the next five days

Now you know how to make proactive, great decisions, over the next five days you need to make one conscious decision a day. Your decision can be as small as 'shall I have tea or coffee?' or as large as you like. Be sure to check the upside and downside carefully. When you make good decisions they become a habit and you are training your brain for when you have larger decisions to make. Write it down so you can keep track of how it works out.

Day One Decision:

_____

Upside: _____

Downside: _____

Day Two Decision:

_____

Upside: _____

Downside: _____

Day Three Decision:

_____

Upside: _____

Downside: _____

Day Four Decision:

_____

Upside: _____

Downside: _____

Day Five Decision:

_____

Upside: _____

Downside: _____

Harness your intuition

Now you have focus and are honing your decision-making skills, we are going to harness the power of your intuition to help your decision-making process become even better. The *Oxford Dictionary* definition of intuition is: 'The ability to understand something instinctively, without the need for conscious reasoning'. And research shows we all have extraordinary intuition – many people just don't use it. Researcher Dr Dean Radin has studied intuition and thought through The Global Consciousness Project, which first started at Princeton University around 1997. He is one of a number of scientists who have studied an extraordinary phenomenon using random number generators. These are electronic coin flippers that have been installed in universities all over the world. When there is an incident of mass consciousness, such as the death of Diana, Princess of Wales, the Super Bowl or the OJ Simpson verdict, astonishingly they go out of a random pattern into an organised pattern.

Dr Radin also tested the limits of the human mind with an intuition experiment where a computer was loaded with a series of images. Some of the photos were calming, such as landscapes and oceans. Others were designed to elicit a negative emotional response, including autopsies. Incredibly, even BEFORE the machine had selected a shocking image, the person tensed up, anticipating it correctly! Before the Boxing Day tsunami of 2004, many of the animals moved inland, which is another example of this phenomenon. So there is overwhelming evidence we've got innate intuition. And this can be harnessed in order to help us to make better decisions.

Another remarkable phenomenon of the largely untapped power of the human mind was demonstrated by research from the Maharishi University of Management. Professor John Hagelin, an expert in quantum physics and transcendental meditation, undertook an extraordinary experiment with a team of fellow scientists aiming to cut crime in Washington, USA. In June 1993, he gathered 4,000 people in the city to meditate, specifically to evoke a sense of peace. The crime rate dropped, according to his calculations, by 18 per cent in a phenomenon he called the 'Peace Field Effect'. It was a demonstration of the extraordinary power of our minds as collective consciousness was able to affect physical reality. It raises fascinating questions about our untapped potential.

Poker players!

Dr Stephen Simpson is a medical doctor who has treated Ebola victims in Africa, and he's now a hypnotherapist, trainer and coach who gets people into 'an enhanced intuition state' so they can make better decisions. Dr Simpson says we have SIX senses that help us to interpret the world around us – so we have an extra one alongside our sight, sound, touch, smell and taste. He says historically we also 'lost' a sixth sense of intuition when we went from being a non-verbal species to talking. He says harnessing your intuition means you can make your own luck! He has coached two of the world's top high-stakes poker players to increase their earnings TENFOLD. But his strategies can be applied to any decision in life.

In his book *The Psychoic Revolution* he says: 'When the conscious mind is quiet, the far more important unconscious mind has room to speak and be heard. Some people call this intuition. If you can develop your intuitive skills the payback can be tremendous. You are then far more likely to experience synchronicities and it is very difficult to explain why this should be so.' He recommends a number of practices including taking time to sit without distractions to give a window for your intuition to speak to you. He also recommends meditating as often as you can (or you can use the hypnotic trance that comes with his book as it is the equivalent of a meditation).

Get even luckier!

Now you have the power to access your intuition, you are about to become more able to boost your own luck! Luck isn't something you were born with. It can be learned and there's science to prove it. You can improve your luck by harnessing the power of a specific part of the brain called the reticular activating system (RAS). The human brain constantly filters the world around us and our RAS is like a heat-seeking missile, which constantly makes adjustments as it flies towards its target or goal. RAS is a network of neurons located in the brain stem and they are a central part of what motivates you. However, the problem is that when people constantly think about what they DON'T want, their mind searches for that, because we get more of what we focus on.

An example of this is that I once cured a woman of a horse phobia after she'd had a bad fall. Her RAS (or perceptual filters) were tuned to spotting horses playing up, and coincidentally she was also a risk analyst in her day job. I was able to get her back in the saddle after explaining to her: 'Your brain is set up to see what could go wrong, and we are going to let you keep that in mind, but we are going to reset it for what could go RIGHT!'

In the same way, you can also harness your RAS to motivate you. For example, you can say: 'I really want this kind of car or this kind of partner.' I did it when I first started out and I really wanted a BMW – I remember I'd see the car I dreamed of everywhere and that spurred me on until I got one of my own! This is because triggering your RAS gives a message to your unconscious mind: 'Notice this, look for this, sort for this,' and you can invest your energy into getting it.

Dr Richard Wiseman has been researching luck for over a decade. He's collected significant evidence that shows that lucky people really do meet their perfect partners, achieve their lifelong ambitions and live happy and meaningful lives. In his book *The Luck Factor* he says lucky people are – often without realising it – guided by their belief in themselves as lucky. This makes them think and behave in ways that create good fortune in their lives as their RAS is constantly filtering for luck! He also found lucky people have four key traits. They notice opportunities when they arise, they listen to their intuition and they are positive and resilient. So lucky people really do make their own luck!

Dr Stephen Simpson also says that simply believing you are lucky makes you luckier. He says: 'Just believing in luck and believing we can all attract more luck into our life becomes in some way a self-fulfilling prophecy, without us having to do much about it.' So believe you are lucky and you will be!

Dr Wiseman did an amazing experiment where both lucky and unlucky people were given a newspaper and he asked them to count the number of photos in it. The unlucky people on average took several minutes but the lucky people took seconds. This was because he'd placed an advert on page two telling them the number of photos. The lucky people's RAS all filtered for luck! But the unlucky ones didn't.

Another great example of this is the legendary hellraiser, Rolling Stone Keith Richards, who has had multiple brushes with death including a car crash, being electrocuted live on stage and falling out of a tree in Fiji. I remember watching an interview with him in the Seventies where Keith was told: 'There's a list in rock 'n' roll of the people most likely to die.' Keith asked if he was on it. The interviewer told him, 'Actually, you are at the top of it.' Keith nonchalantly puffed on his cigarette and replied: 'I'll let you know how I get on. My luck hasn't run out yet.'

As I watched that interview I had a revelation that luck may be an energy. That has led me to develop a Luck Generator technique, which I initially tried on a group of ten people and every one of them had a massive turn of good luck. Some instantly had massive breakthroughs in their business, others in their relationships, etc. However, some people had to clear out the bad people, the crooks or vampires, so the lucky energy could thrive, so the process involved a little discomfort before massive success. When I tried the Luck Generator technique in my own life, I had to personally get rid of two awful people. Initially I had no idea that they were vampires, who brought negativity to my life. But once I realised, I cut ties and my life improved immeasurably.

While it takes just a few minutes to do, if you want me to guide you, then you can listen to the audio that goes with this book. Let's supercharge your luck now!

THE LUCK GENERATOR

🔊 Please read through this technique first, before you do it, or even better click on the audio and I will personally guide you through it.

1. Remember a time when you felt lucky or at least that everything was going your way. Remember it vividly, like you are back there again now. See what you saw, hear what you heard, and feel how good you felt.

2. Now, make the images in your mind, the memory of the images, bigger; the colours brighter, bolder, richer; the sounds louder and the feelings stronger.

3. Keep going through the memory again and again, over and over until you feel really, really good!

4. Now, notice where you feel the good feeling strongest in your body. It could be in your chest, heart or somewhere else.

continued

5. Next, give that good feeling a colour and spread that colour up to the top of your head and down to the tip of your toes. Take time to do it now.

6. Next, double the brightness and intensity of the colour and feeling and double it again and again, until you feel it in every fibre of your being!

7. Now, take the colour and feeling to its absolute maximum, 100 per cent.

8. Now take it 120 per cent, 130 per cent, now 140 per cent …

9. Now take it to a million, billion, trillion per cent stronger. Make the colour bright, bold and the feeling strong.

10. While you have that amazing feeling at a strong level, imagine spreading it to every area of your life. Send your luck energy into your health, relationships and love, money, career, and lifestyle and happiness. Imagine sending it through every one of those cornerstones of your life and way off into your future.

Right now, you should be glowing with good feelings and positive luck energy. Do this technique every day and notice how your life changes for the better.

HOLLYWOOD MANIFESTOR

Hollywood megastar Arnold Schwarzenegger visualises success. He has said: 'If I can see it, then it must be a reality. And I can make it a reality. So it is only then a matter of following through with the work.' It's taken him from bodybuilder to global superstar and politician!

Five seconds can change your life

Now you've enhanced your focus, decision-making, luck and intuition, it's time to build momentum to propel you to where you want to be. Some people get stuck in their head instead of taking action. You can stay in your mind trying to figure things out forever. Or you can follow these techniques and then GO FOR IT!

With that in mind, I want you to consider these two questions. If you are still a little sceptical about manifestation and you think it's really just all about action, then ask yourself this:

Are you taking the actions that will bring you what you want?

Conversely, if you believe action is all a load of nonsense and it's all down to frequency, energy and the universe, then you need to ask yourself this question:

Are you using your mind in a way that would bring what you want to you?

For instance, if you had a great idea for a product or service and six months later you walked into a store or went online and you saw someone else had done it, the difference between you and them is they took action, and you didn't.

Richard Branson once told me that he designed Virgin Airlines when he was on a flight in the Seventies. There was one television in the centre of the plane that no one could see, someone threw down something resembling chicken as the in-flight meal, and overall it wasn't a great experience. So, he asked himself a genius question: 'If I had an airline, what would I do?' He decided he'd give everyone their own TV and high-quality headset to enjoy in-flight entertainment; he would create a lounge you looked forward to going to. He also decided he'd put a bar on the plane for people to gather and he'd make the seats really comfortable. He invented a category that was between business and first class called 'upper class', redefining air travel.

After he got off the flight where he had designed his airline of the future, he took action and rang Boeing. He said: 'How much is it for one of your jumbo jets?' To buy one could have bankrupted him as it was so expensive. So he asked: 'Could we lease it from you?' And they said, 'Yes.' So he reduced the risk by leasing his company's first jumbo and then he took MASSIVE ACTION. Apparently, at the end of the phone call the bloke from Boeing said: 'What did you say the name of your company is again? Virgin? We've never heard of you.' And at the time, other airline executives said: 'What can someone from the entertainment industry possibly offer the airline industry?' Well, apparently everything!

What Richard Branson's success encapsulates is an important rule in making money. It is that:

We get paid for adding value.

For example, if you create something that makes people's lives easier, you get rewarded. However, technically it's not just adding value, but 'perceived' value. For example, supermodels are paid more than doctors, because they are a scarcer resource. Richard Branson was adding value because he was making the experience of flying far more enjoyable. His concepts, including personal entertainment with a TV in every seat, were revolutionary at the time. These innovations suddenly made Virgin the best choice for flying and it wasn't long before the entire industry followed suit. He not only offered what everyone else was offering, he did it way better. His airline was only a fraction of the size of the other major airlines but he changed history by being a trailblazer.

One of America's greatest commanders, General George S. Patton, once said: 'A good plan violently executed now is better than a perfect plan executed next week.' When an idea comes or is presented to me, once I've filtered through the process of upside and downside, Cleaned and Cleared it and got the feeling of 'Yes!' then I'm on the phone getting on with it. My whole mindset is then one of 'Let's go!'

An incredibly powerful tool to get you going and spur you into action is one that takes just FIVE SECONDS! The author of *The 5 Second Rule* Mel Robbins has created the simplest formula that has transformed lives all over the globe. She says in her TED Talk that far too many people convince themselves they are 'fine' with their lot – but 'fine' crushes too many dreams. This, ultimately, can lead people to feel stuck. She says the feeling of being stuck doesn't mean you are broken, but it signals that one of your basic needs isn't being met. But by taking action you can change that. She says: 'Getting what you want is simple. Notice I didn't say it was easy ... If you have one of those little impulses that are pulling you, if you don't marry it with an action within five seconds, you pull the emergency brake and kill the idea.' Her 'five second rule' is the antidote to this and will spring you into action. Count backwards from 5, 4, 3, 2, 1, then tell yourself 'Go!' And do it!

POWER MANIFESTING IN ACTION

It's important to start small and build up. Mel says the first decision many people make every morning is to roll over, press the snooze button and stay in bed. So from tomorrow set your alarm for 30 minutes earlier and, when your alarm goes off, get straight out of bed and get on with your day. The force of that one action, she says, is the same amount of force as that needed to change your other behaviours and therefore your entire life. So five seconds is all you need to change everything. The power of this is illustrated by the legendary mountaineer William Hutchison Murray, who once said:

> Until one is committed, there is hesitancy, the chance to draw back, always ineffectiveness. Concerning all acts of initiative (and creation) there is one elementary truth, the ignorance of which kills countless ideas and splendid plans: that the moment one definitely commits oneself, then Providence moves too.

The idea that when you move into a state of action, then the world moves with you, is something I also live by.

Let's try it now. What is a small decision you could make at this moment? Tea or coffee? What should you watch tonight on TV? What is something you are going to do in terms of career or relationships? **5, 4, 3, 2, 1 – Go!**

Once you have got going, and set your plan into action, momentum will soon start to build. My friend Michael Neill, author of *Creating the Impossible*, says: 'Momentum is the ultimate force multiplier for success.' He says to think of gaining momentum with anything you want to achieve as being like the wheels turning on a bike. At first, it takes a lot of effort to get it going. But once the wheels are spinning there comes a tipping point where it's easier to keep going than to stop. He says: 'With each turn it moves faster, then at some point – you can't say exactly when – you break through. The momentum kicks in. It spins faster and faster with its own weight propelling it. You aren't pushing any harder but it's accelerating, it's momentum building … it's speed increasing.'

MUSICAL MANIFESTOR

Three-time Grammy Award winner Olivia Rodrigo previously told Jimmy Fallon how she has manifested her career. At just six years old she had a pop star-themed party that even had a set list of songs. She said: 'There was no audience, no one was watching, but I had all of my kindergarten friends and we were just singing the Jonas Brothers. We were really into it.'

Using your internal timeline to Power Manifest

Now you have gained focus, honed your decision-making, luck and intuition skills, and embraced taking action and gaining momentum, you will now harness the superpower of your internal timeline. This is the process by which you will Power Manifest going forward.

First we need to understand how you code the past, present and future in your internal timeline. Everybody has a way of coding and thinking about time and events in relation to each other. When I think about an event next week I visualise it in front of me and a few inches away from my face in my mind's eye. When I think about an event I'm doing in three months time, that is further ahead of me. When I think about something six months away, that's three feet ahead of me. If I think about my last birthday, it's behind me. So for me, the future in my internal timeline extends out in front and the past is behind me. Other people have the past on their left, the present moment right in front of them and the future to their right. Some people have it go round them in a circle and others have it curve off in a direction or up and down. There is no right or wrong way to code time and everybody is different. The easy way to discover how you code time is to think of something you know is happening next week, next month and in six months and you will have a sense of the direction, and that's all you really need to know.

We are going to harness your internal timeline to set your dreams in motion. Remember, when there is an event that we know is going to happen, it appears on our timeline as images or movies. But there's a neat thing you can do – you can transform the brain so it puts into your future timeline events you WANT to happen, too. This tricks the subconscious mind into believing it's an inevitability. It then organises all your thinking, behaviours and all your focus to make it happen. That is the difference that can make all the difference. So you will go off into the future where you've attained your dream and stack it with an amazing future life vision. Then you will step back in increments and find out how you got there. This is an incredibly potent way to achieve way beyond what you may currently believe is possible. It gives your conscious and unconscious mind a road map to get you there.

Let's do it now with your dreams. Remember, I can talk you through this process step by step with the audio that accompanies this book.

HARNESS YOUR INTERNAL TIMELINE

🔊 Please read through this technique first, before you do it, or even better click on the audio and I will personally guide you through it.

1. Close your eyes if it's safe to do so.

2. Now, imagine floating out down the timeline one year from now.

3. Next, imagine it's been one of the best years of your life, where the **five dreams** you wrote down earlier have happened. What do you see, hear and feel?

4. If it's been one of the best years of your life, what must have happened in regard to your **health** (both mental and physical), **relationships and love** (both personal and professional), your **finances**, your **career**, your **spiritual life** and, finally, your general levels of **happiness**?

5   Get a real sense of how amazing your life is. What do you see, hear and feel?

6   What are the things that let you know your life is great?

7   Keep going over them. Now live an ideal day in your perfect future.

8   Now, keeping all the good feelings with you, step out of this future and make it a cinema screen-sized image on your timeline. See your optimised self on the big screen, looking healthy, happy and successful.

9   Now float back from that successful you, one year from now, in stages. First, float back three months earlier on the timeline and get a sense of what happened and make an image of yourself looking healthy, happy and successful.

continued

10. Next, float back another three months earlier on the timeline and get a sense of what happened then and make an image of yourself looking healthy, happy and successful.

11. Float back three months earlier again on the timeline and get a sense of what happened then and make an image of yourself looking healthy, happy and successful.

12. Now float all the way back to now. You will be able to see a succession of images of you looking healthy, happy and successful. As the images move further away they get bigger; the image one year from now is massive like a cinema screen, with you on it and all the people you love, and everything you know that makes you see your life is amazing will be big, bright, bold and wonderful.

Now, remember to look at this succession of images every day to Power Manifest the direction of your life going forward.

POWER MANIFESTING IN ACTION

MUSIC MANIFESTOR

Before she became famous, Lady Gaga used affirmations. In an interview in 2011 she said: 'You repeat it to yourself every day. And it's not [true] yet, it's a lie. You're saying a lie over and over again, and then one day the lie is true.'

POWER MANIFESTING IN ACTION

Take a moment to give yourself a massive pat on the back, as you are now a Power Manifestor! You now have all the tools you need to transform your life going forward, dream by dream. Extraordinary change is already underway and your life is going to get better than you ever imagined before. But if you wish, it's not over yet, and you can move straight on to Advanced Power Manifesting in the next section. Or you can stop here and put your dream Power Manifesting to the test. The choice is yours.

If it's the latter, then I'd like you to jump to page 186 where there's one last process to reinforce the techniques you've learned. You can then return to the questions you filled in at the start of the book and see how much you've already changed in the few hours it's taken you to read this book and do the techniques. BUT, if you are up for more, in the next section you can learn the secrets of Advanced Power Manifesting, which will take specific areas of your life STRATOSPHERIC and deepen your skill set. So let's go!

Section Three
Advanced Power Manifesting

Now you have begun the process to Power Manifest your five dream areas of your life, you will be feeling fantastic. In this bonus section we are going to take things QUANTUM with Advanced Power Manifesting, which will enhance your skill set in specific areas of your life.

When I've asked people in the past: 'What's your ambition for the future?', they have said things like: 'I don't know...' Or, 'I've got a number in my head I want to earn.' This section will help you to Power Manifest a BIGGER and BRIGHTER life picture. In addition, I will introduce you to some of the more spiritual aspects of manifesting too.

How it works

You have the choice to focus on five of the things people most often want to Power Manifest. These are **health**, **relationships and love**, **money**, **career** and **lifestyle and happiness**. While ultimately I suggest you go through all five techniques, to begin with, choose the one that appeals to you most and start there. So, if you want to Power Manifest cash flooding into your life, jump straight to Power Manifesting Money. Maybe you've already got love so instead you want to improve your career, so then you'd start there. You can pick and choose what works for you.

Even if you feel you are already successful in any of these areas I recommend that you still do each of the processes as it will make things EVEN BETTER! You also have the opportunity to do a potent healing process for your Karma.

The spiritual side of manifesting

First, I want to introduce you to the spiritual side of manifesting. This quote, often attributed to one of the most influential writers of all time, Johann Wolfgang von Goethe, is one I live by:

Be bold and mighty forces will come to your aid.

Take a second to think about how there are so many things that defy a definitive explanation. For instance, if you ask a philosopher for their definition of love and then ask a neuroscientist, you will get two answers that are both true, but completely different. A neuroscientist will tell you there's a sequence of neurotransmitters and electricity that takes place when someone feels love or attraction to another person. A philosopher might describe love as a means by which our 'self' and our world is affected once we are 'touched by love' and it's something that goes beyond physical attraction to a deep emotional connection. So there's no definitive answer! Yet most of us have experienced love in some form, and there is overwhelming evidence that people fall in love because just look around!

Another extraordinary example of something that defies a concrete explanation is a bizarre phenomenon called Stendhal moments. This is where people suffer dizzy spells and massive emotional overwhelm and become disoriented after seeing art of great beauty. It was first described by the 19th-century French author Stendhal, whose real name was Marie-Henri Beyle. Yet, in the 21st century, hospital staff in Florence are reportedly accustomed to seeing tourists suffering from it after viewing the abundance of astonishing art in the city. I personally find it extraordinary that people can find something so beautiful that they faint. However, I totally understand feeling emotionally overwhelmed at beautiful music, sunsets or moments of pure intimacy. So a similar experience is when we say; 'I am overwhelmed' or 'I'm speechless', when something strikes us profoundly.

Similar to Stendhal moments is the magic of Disney's 'wonderment' for children. Back in the Eighties I was a voiceover artist as well as a DJ and one day I went to do a Disney commercial. I remember stepping inside a recording booth and saying: 'The wonderful world of Disney.' The producer said, 'Step out of the booth, sir. Could you give it more wonderment?' When I asked what he meant he explained: 'Do you remember as a child opening your presents on Christmas morning?' I said, 'Yes!' He continued, 'Do you remember the first time you rode a bike by yourself?' I said, 'Yes!' He added, 'Do you remember the first time you saw a plane take off?' I said, 'Yes!' He said, 'Well, that's "wonderment".' I went back into the booth and nailed it.

Something else that defies a definitive explanation is something close to my heart – hypnosis! I know that hypnosis works but there are three schools of thought as to why and no one has been able to fully explain it. One theory is that it's a special state of being, a second is that it's social compliance and the third is there's no baseline for what normal, waking consciousness is. It might be an altered state but altered from what? You can't have a baseline of normal, waking consciousness as everybody is different! So one person's normal, waking consciousness is another person's trance, in a sense. But what I can do is tell you that hypnosis works.

Perhaps down the line scientists will be able to fully understand the secrets of manifesting – just like scientists cracked the genetic code. Once upon a time, entomologists said that a bumblebee's flight was impossible due to its physics-defying aerodynamics, based on the assumption that it flapped its wings up and down. It was later found the flapping happens back and forth, a bit like a partial spin of a helicopter propeller. It was once claimed by eminent scientists that rocks can't fall from the sky, but we know of meteorites; and it was even once claimed by great scientific minds that if trains went more than 40 mph then everyone would suffocate!

So while at the moment I cannot tell you exactly how manifesting works, or even prove its existence, the results – just like being hypnotised, or the immensely powerful emotion of true love – are overwhelming. The reason I'm telling you this is because I want you to open your mind as we now explore the more spiritual side of Power Manifesting.

SPORTING MANIFESTOR

Olympic runner Keely Hodgkinson was left partially deaf in one ear and temporarily unable to walk following a tumour in her teens yet won gold at Paris 2024. She told the *High Performance Podcast*: 'I'm quite a visualising person. So for me, I think to get into that mindset, it would just be like: "What's it going to feel like winning that gold?"'

The power of your Karma

When it comes to manifesting, the debate often moves to Karma and the Law of Attraction and their influence. The Law of Attraction suggests the more you think and feel about something, the more likely it is to come into your life. There's something to be said for this, as angry people find other angry people and rich people find other rich ones (as illustrated by the Law of Sympathetic Resonance, which I described earlier in this book). As for Karma, broadly speaking, Western philosophy says that if you do good things, good things happen to you. (You reap what you sow.)

However, why is it that good people get cancer and villains have superyachts? While there is certainly some truth in that if you are nice to people most will be nice back, I support an Eastern philosophy of Karma, which is that 'you pull to you life lessons you need to learn'. If I think of the worst things that have happened to me, there has been a learning or a benefit and I've grown as a person, no matter how hard it was at the time. There is no black or white answer to this and I don't have a definitive answer. But that is how I make sense of the world.

The big question I've always wanted answered is: 'Can you affect your Karma through a visualisation?' And I believe you can. Years ago I did this extraordinary process and it helped to change my destiny. That doesn't mean I no longer have problems and challenges. I do, and life still isn't always fair. But I believe this technique is a game changer. I then did it with a group of ten people over a period of a few weeks and every one of them had massive, profound and positive life changes.

A simple way to visualise your Karma is as an energy field that surrounds you. I'd like you to try it now. Close your eyes and notice what it looks like. It will have a colour. Note what it is. (There is no right or wrong answer as everyone is different.) When you visualise your Karma, it's important to see if there are any cracks, holes, dark spaces or anything that doesn't feel good. When I first did this I noticed I had some dark spaces and cracks down the bottom left-hand side. The idea with this is to make your aura beautiful and bright and to get it to feel good. This gives a message to your unconscious mind, and arguably the universe, that you are changing your energy and frequency. Without exception, when people fill in the cracks and dark spaces they feel massively uplifted.

I recommend you spend a few minutes as often as you can – and if possible daily – doing this, as I believe you can change your Karma. If you'd like me to talk you through it step by step, you can listen to the audio now. And don't worry about getting it wrong. When any cracks, holes or dark spaces are filled in, you will know you are changing your Karma for the better as it will feel really good.

CHANGE YOUR KARMA

🔊 Please read through this technique first, before you do it, or even better click on the audio and I will personally guide you through it.

1. When you think of your Karma, notice what image comes to mind. Is it like an energy field around you or something else? Notice how you represent the karmic field around you. What colour is it?

2. Notice if there are any holes, cracks or dark spots.

3. Now with the colour of your positive Karma, fill in any holes or cracks and disperse any dark spots with the positive Karma colour.

4. Now, brighten up the colour of your positive karmic field around your body. Make it bold, bright and positive.

5. Now open your eyes and see how you feel.

CELEBRITY MANIFESTOR

Supermodel Kendall Jenner has said: 'I don't chase, I attract. What's meant for me will simply find me.' She wrote a letter to herself aged 14 saying that her goal was to be a successful model.

Using the power of your neuro-coding

Now that you have optimised your Karma, you can Power Manifest the cornerstones of **health, relationships and love, money, career** and **lifestyle and happiness**. You can choose how many of these you would like to do. So you can do just one, or you can do them ALL!

You will discover, as you Power Manifest them, that other aspects of your life will start to fall into place. For instance, there's an American success coach and her sole focus is on getting female entrepreneurs to boost their earning power. Yet, she revealed there is an unexpected side effect. When her clients start making money they all lose weight! The human psyche is an interdependent system, so if you optimise one thing it almost always has a positive domino effect on other aspects of your life too! So let's take things to another level!

Power Manifesting health

In this section we are going to Power Manifest health. The mind and body are linked in a cybernetic loop where one is always influencing the other. Scientists have proven the power of your mind can profoundly influence your health.

An extraordinary experiment done by Harvard psychologist Ellen Langer created real-life Benjamin Buttons – people who aged in reverse! In 1979, eight residential home residents volunteered to go to a retreat where everything was set up as if it was 1959. They were asked to behave as if they were two decades younger, as she wanted to find out whether there would be an accompanying physical change if the clock were turned back psychologically. There were no mirrors, and they even put up portraits of the residents when they were 20 years younger so that they visualised themselves as their younger selves. Within just a week, Dr Langer found they had all de-aged! She later wrote in her book *Counter Clockwise* that 60 per cent of them had better intelligence-test scores than at the start of the experiment, and that they had better physical strength, posture and even vision. It illustrates that what you believe really can have a dramatic impact.

Dr Joe Dispenza, author of *Evolve Your Brain*, studies an emerging field called epigenetics, which explores how behaviours and environment can cause changes to the body. He also supports the idea that the power of your mind can have a massive impact on your physical health – and he has undertaken a study that proves an attitude of gratitude can boost your immune system. He studied 120 people in Tacoma, Washington by measuring their levels of cortisol (a stress hormone) and immunoglobulin A (a blood protein that is part of your immune system) to give a baseline of their immunity. Then, over the course of four days, they all spent ten minutes, three times a day focusing on high-frequency states of love, joy and gratitude. Incredibly, his study found overall their cortisol levels dropped and their igA levels rose. So gratitude boosted their immune systems! Dr Dispenza has previously said: 'Something as simple as moving into an elevated state of joy, love or gratitude for five to ten minutes a day can produce significant epigenetic changes in our health and bodies.'

And he's not alone in his belief. Study upon study has shown that going into a positive neurophysiological state can boost immunity. Researchers at the universities of Utah and Kentucky found that optimistic students had more disease-fighting cells in their bodies. Robert A. Emmons, a professor of psychology at the University of California, Davis, has said physical effects of gratitude include lower blood pressure, better sleep and immune-system-boosting abilities. So, put simply:

The practice of gratitude can have dramatic and lasting effects in a person's life.

This fascinating field falls within the field of psychoneuro-immunology (PNI). When you are in fear, stress and hatred, you produce a set of fight-or-flight chemicals. Lactic acid and adrenaline flood your system, your immune system is suppressed and blood is pumped to the major limbs so you can fight or run away. In our modern world of work and family pressures, your fight-or-flight reaction is triggered all day long to some extent. We can get rid of these stress toxins by exercising or through deep relaxation (including meditation) or hypnosis. But we can also redress the balance by having a mindset of gratitude as an antidote. When you move out of a stressed state and into concentrated periods of gratitude, not only are you rebooting your immune system (as your body is no longer in fight-or-flight mode), but you also affirm at the subconscious level 'I'm abundant, I am enough', so your frequency is boosted too. So gratitude doesn't just make you a better person, it really is good for you!

Cell biologist Dr Bruce Lipton also argues that psychology plays a pivotal role in our health and wellbeing. He has argued that our thoughts transmit to our cells and this can lead to physiological changes. He has said: 'The latest discoveries in science reveal that our perception plays a powerful role in shaping our biology. We now know that we are not mere victims of our genes or external forces. Instead, we are active participants in creating our health, behaviour and life experiences.' This is based around a concept, that our genes are not the sole determinant of our health – our behaviour and lifestyle are key too. An extraordinary example of this in action is a friend of mine who was age-regressed. He'd been previously hit by shrapnel when he was serving in the military and, when he was taken back to that time, a bruise appeared where he'd been hit.

Now we've explored the fact that thought can impact our health either positively or negatively, we're going to put it into action. In order to Power Manifest good health you've got to regularly see yourself fit, well and happy in your future. You extend do this by harnessing your internal timeline.

When I talk to some people about their future, their internal timeline does not extend far enough. So first, you need to lay some extra track down and extend it! I did this early on in my career as a therapist after I had a conversation with a fellow NLP therapist where I said: 'The problem with getting older is you get decrepit and get bad health.' My friend said, 'Wow, Paul, that's really interesting that you've got that to look forward to.' In a split second I said, 'You are absolutely right! When I thought about my future back then I saw myself getting steadily unhealthier.' I realised that was effectively installing the equivalent of really bad manifesting. So I changed it. Now I have installed a vision of myself looking happy, healthy and fit for the next 40 years – taking me to 100 years old. By changing my thoughts I've influenced my behaviour to look after my health in a better way than before.

Now you are going to step into your future, healthy self. You will visualise the healthy life you will be leading in the future and float into it. You will experience what it feels like when you feel healthier with a mindset of balance and moderation. Then we are going to stretch out the timeline of your life to when you are healthy a week from now, a month from now, then five years, ten years, 20 years, to 40 years and beyond. When you visualise yourself healthy and happy make the pictures bright and bold, as this says to your unconscious mind: 'Make that happen.' Obviously we are all going to die, as everybody does, but psychologically you are stacking the odds in your favour to enjoy your best possible life.

Go to the audio that accompanies this book if you want me to take you through it step by step. Let's try it now.

BOOST YOUR HEALTH

🔊 Please read through this technique first, before you do it, or even better click on the audio and I will personally guide you through it.

1 Close your eyes and imagine there's a cinema screen in front of you.

2 On that screen, see a movie of super-healthy you.

continued

---

3 Look at your posture and expression.

4 Look at how the healthy version of you moves and gestures.

5 Look at the way you radiate really great health.

6 Now float into that healthy you, see through the eyes of your healthy self, hear your internal dialogue say, 'I am healthy', and notice how good you feel.

7 Notice where you feel the good feeling strongest in your body.

8 Next, give that good feeling a colour.

9 Now, imagine moving that colour up into your neck and head and down into your shoulders and chest. Finally, move the colour into your legs and feet, until you are glowing with health.

> 10 While feeling this healthy, imagine travelling a week into the future, then a month, then a year, then two years, five years, ten years, 20 years, 30 years, 40 years and so on …

Congratulations, you have Power Manifested your ultimate vision of **health**. If you wish (or haven't already), you can Power Manifest **relationships and love**, **money**, **career** or **lifestyle and happiness**, too.

Power Manifesting relationships and love

In Greek mythology there is a beautiful concept around love where you spend your life searching for the other half of you. According to legend, the god Zeus feared humans, who back then had four arms and four legs. So in order to make them less powerful, he cut them in two so the two halves spent the rest of their lives searching for each other. That's how I think of my relationship with Kate, my wife – she completes me. So let's manifest relationships and love.

In this section you are going to use the super-powerful process of Havening for the third time – this time to open your heart to love. I have chosen to use it three times in this book as you are looking for a result – and remember, Havening is the most powerful technique for instantly dissolving psychological and energetic blocks. Then, you'll use a series of strategies to boost your self-love and help make your relationships more functional. Even if you are already in a committed relationship, this can make things even better!

A lot of people think of relationships as a destination. Often people think being with someone is the finish line, or as a 'thing', almost as though you could put it in a wheelbarrow. But a relationship is not a 'thing', it's a constantly changing, dynamic process. That means adaptability is at the core of a functional and healthy one! Also, it is not what you dream, or wish for, or hope for – it is what actually HAPPENS that defines a relationship! So what's most important is what we DO!

In addition, this is the antidote to any self-hatred or lack of self-worth in relationships. Negative messages that people have experienced in their formative years mean many people think they might not be 'enough'. We are also bombarded with social media influencers and commercials where everyone is slimmer, more beautiful, richer and apparently more fabulous – and it can leave many people feeling a lack of self-worth and lead to emotional scarring. Latest figures reveal 61 per cent of ten- to 17-year-old girls in the UK have low self-esteem (source: www.theyarethefuture.co.uk).

The power of Havening is backed up by a mountain of scientific proof. Sometimes I meet critics who say: 'There's no scientific evidence that Havening works' and I ask them how they know. They usually say: 'I read it on the internet.' Their claim usually ends in slight embarrassment when I produce all the scientific studies that have been conducted over more than a decade that show it works brilliantly for treating stress, PTSD, trauma, pain and removing blocks.

So if you want to remove any blocks to you receiving love into your life, you will love this two-part technique. The first part removes blocks. The second part boosts your inner love – as you have to love yourself in order to love someone else. Let's try it now.

BOOST YOUR ABILITY TO RECEIVE LOVE

🔊 Please read through this technique first, before you do it, or even better click on the audio and I will personally guide you through it.

PART ONE

1. Close your eyes and summon any feelings or fear of being disliked, self-loathing, un-loveability, feeling not worthy or even self-hatred.

2. Rate them on a scale of 1 to 10.

3. Put your right hand on your left shoulder and your left hand on your right shoulder.

4. Begin gently stroking the sides of your arms from the top of your shoulder to your elbow. Continue to do this throughout this process.

5. When the uncomfortable feelings are at their peak, clear your mind.

continued

6. Now, imagine you are walking on a beach and with each footstep in the sand count out loud from 1 to 20.

7. Next, remember a time when you felt really happy and return to it again like you are back there again now. Make the colours rich and bold, the sounds loud and the feelings strong.

8. Notice where the feelings are strongest in your body and give them a colour.

9. Now imagine moving that colour up to the top of your head and down to the tips of your toes, so you are bathed in that colour.

10. Still stroking the sides of your arms, imagine walking in a garden and count out loud from 1 to 20 with each footstep you take.

11. Now stop and notice how much the uncomfortable feelings have reduced and how much better you feel.

PART TWO

1. Keep stroking the sides of your arms and with your eyes closed imagine you can see a cinema screen in front of you.

2. On the screen watch a movie of a loveable you; someone who naturally connects with others, a friendly, happy you that radiates joy and love. Notice your posture, expression and manner. Notice the way you interact with other people and the world. Notice the light behind your eyes, the sound of your voice, and everything that lets you know you are loveable.

3. When the movie of you looks really good, float into the screen and into yourself. See through the eyes of your more confident self, hear your internal dialogue and feel how good it feels.

4. Notice where the feelings are strongest in your body and give them a colour. *continued*

> 5. Now imagine moving that colour up to the top of your head and down to the tips of your toes, so you are bathed in that colour.
>
> 6. Imagine taking that colour and feeling with you into all the environments of your life. What will you see, hear and feel as you are glowing with this wonderful colour that lets you know you are loveable?

Now we have cleared the way for more love, it's time to make your relationships more functional. Broadly speaking, there are three types of partner: **visual** (they like to see things such as a bunch of flowers, a present or an act of service); **auditory** (I am of this type – they like to hear 'I love you' or 'I miss you' etc.); and finally **kinaesthetic**, which relates to feeling (they need reassurance with touch – words alone are not enough). While you may have a bit of each, there will be one dominant trait. So you need to identify your partner (and yourself) in order to feel safe and secure in any relationship you enter into.

THE TEN THINGS THAT MAKE OR BREAK A RELATIONSHIP

One of my mentors, Lieutenant General Sir Graeme Lamb, the former Director of Special Forces, once said to me: 'There are ultimately only two big decisions in life: "Who are you going to partner with?" and "How are you going to die?" The rest is noise.' We all inherit ideas and habits we have not consciously or unconsciously chosen that shape our relationships. Sometimes we create them to protect ourselves and later on find those same habits cause problems.

The reason I was single for years is because I'd had my heart broken and so I was a commitment-phobe. I would tell myself a story: 'I'm not trapped in one of those relationships' or 'I'm happily single' and it was all about pleasure and not about happiness. But actually a part of me did want to be happy in a relationship. For others, when they are growing up, how their parents interact with each other is like a training video. So we tend to become like one of our parents in terms of relationship dynamics. Then, if for some reason it doesn't work out, we often take on the role of our other parent in our next relationship. This is how people can unconsciously repeat the same kind of relationship patterns over and over again.

With any relationship you enter into, there are ten things that you should consider in order to make it healthy and functional. They are:

1. Communication – The first question you should ask of any relationship is: 'What is this person's motivation? Are they seeking pleasure or are they seeking happiness?' Remember any relationship has two people, therefore two perspectives, and it's an ongoing conversation.

2. Invest time, effort and action – Your relationship is what happens. You can make it happen every day.

3. Self-care – You can only love someone functionally if you learn to love yourself. One of the big errors people make is to think of their partner but not themselves.

4 Have a loving mindset – Love can be understood in many different ways, but it includes giving your time and emotions. Even small acts of service, like making a cup of tea, help to build a relationship.

5 Disagree healthily – Some conflict over time is inevitable. It's how you work together so both of you feel heard that counts. Rather than go straight to battle stations or passive-aggressive silent treatment, sometimes it's OK to agree to disagree.

6 Learn – We can constantly learn from each other, our environment and ourselves. Be open to this. Remember to also ask your partner, 'What do you want or need in order for our relationship to flourish?'

7 Have a vision of the future – The energy of a relationship flows best when it moves towards a destination that inspires us. This helps in hard times as well as good ones.

continued

8   Avoid personal criticism of your partner, including during conflict resolution. For example, let us imagine Jane says: 'Let's go on holiday to Greece next year,' and John replies: 'Maybe we should think about somewhere more local'; how you deal with this is key to a relationship's long-term success. If Jane says, 'You are so negative!' then the discussion is no longer about holiday plans. It's now a personal criticism. Instead, she should ask him what his specific worry is in order to resolve the difference of opinion.

9   Pay attention to your partner. Your attention is one of the most powerful gifts you have. It demonstrates your respect, helps you to understand them better and notice small but important differences in what they say, helps them to discover more about themselves and enables you to share deeper moments of intimacy.

> 10 If you are in a relationship, return in your mind to some of the happiest times as if you are there again – reinforcing the positives. This helps you fall even more in love. If you are not in a relationship, imagine the wonderful things you would do with your new partner, including places you would go, people you would see and all the wonderful things you would do together.

It's also important NOT to look to a partner to give you happiness. You have to be happy in yourself to be able to form a functional relationship. This was proven in a groundbreaking study in Germany in 2003, which found that people who are happily married tend to be happy before they get hitched. So being happy in yourself is the best predictor of a long and successful relationship. That's exactly what happened to me. When I was unhappy I kept creating short relationships. When I was finally truly happy within myself, I found Kate.

It's also important to acknowledge that not everyone is looking for their 'other half'. In today's dating landscape, there are many shapes and sizes of relationships from marital partners to long-term companions to lovers or even friends with benefits. But it's good to have a functional mindset however your relationship looks.

OPEN YOUR HEART TO LOVE

Love is all you need, according to the lyrics of the Beatles song, and now you've cleared any relationship blocks, and have strategies to make it work optimally, it's time to open your heart to love. Dr Robert Holden, author of *Loveability*, says connecting with love will enrich everything. He said: 'Love is the real work of your life. As you release the blocks to love you flourish even more in your relationships, work and life. In some ways, love is the master key. All roads lead to love.'

Many people are tempted to give up on love, as they have experienced heartbreak. But one of Dr Holden's principal teachings is:

Love has never hurt you.

There is a very important distinction to be made here. It's not *love* that hurts you, it's when people are *unloving* that you get hurt. This is very important to understand, as you can't manifest something you are afraid of. So if you say you want love, but it scares you, then you are less likely to get it. Instead, you may end up with a nice consolation prize, which is dreaming that you might find love one day. But that's not the same thing! Dr Holden also says:

To open your heart to love, you must be willing to become the most loving person you can be.

If you want to love *somebody* you have got to embrace a loving mindset with *everybody*. Love doesn't pick and choose. You can't decide you're going to be super-loving to one person and more emotionally distant with everyone else. Dr Holden recommends starting your loving mindset by making a conscious effort to be present, to connect with people and embrace small acts of service. For example, notice if somebody could benefit from your smile today or hold a door open for a stranger. The more loving acts you can do, the better. This affirms at an unconscious level that you are a loving person and it also raises your frequency to love. Remember, manifesting is always happening. We can manifest anxiety, positivity, fear … and love! You don't become a manifestor, you already are one. But you are just choosing to get more of what you focus on.

Love is everywhere. But Dr Holden says: 'Looking for love makes you neurotic; being a loving person makes you sane again.' So it's not so much about *finding or searching for* it, it's more about being *open* to it, recognising it, being willing to give the very thing that you are looking for. The 'finding' idea should simply be an intention, which is to experience more love. But, in the end, we have to be willing to *be* the love that we are looking for. Because if you are willing to give it, *like attracts like*. He says: 'So when somebody says, "I'm looking for love," I'll say you've got to step things up, and become the most loving person that you can be. You need to be brave.'

Of course, manifesting love would be a great deal easier if none of us had a past. Many of us have scars from being heartbroken, disappointed, or having suffered a betrayal or perhaps the loss of a loved one. Even if past relationships have failed, Dr Holden says: 'If someone is in your life, it is because they have a gift for you and you have a gift for them.' So, if you really want to manifest love (or anything else for that matter), you must be willing to *forgive the past*. You must be willing to have a new relationship with your history – one where you can look back on it with wisdom, while acknowledging that it does not absolutely define you – as you still have a life to live.

If you feel at all stuck, in order to move forward, you need to ask yourself this question:

**Am I going to choose my story
or am I going to choose 'possibility'?**

So, have a little pep talk with yourself and ask: is your future only a repeat of the past or is it possible that you could surprise yourself here? After all, this time around, with the maturity of who you are today and some of the inner work you've already done, along with your wisdom – maybe now is the time when it could go a lot better than it did before?

So now it's time to ask yourself two further key questions. On his Loveability Programme, Dr Holden conducts a poll with his students at the start of a module called 'The Mirror Principle'. The poll consists of two statements you decide are either true or false. These are:

> 1. It is easier to love others than it is to love yourself.
>
> 2. The more you love yourself, the easier it is to love others.

Ask yourself these questions now. Interestingly, most students say both statements are true. So how can this be? Well, it serves as an eye opener. The first statement is a myth. Dr Holden explains that perhaps a better way of saying it is: *The less well we love ourselves, the more difficult it is for others to love us.* When it comes to relationships, in the honeymoon stage there is no difficulty. One of the reasons is because we are in the *present*, not thinking about the past, so any doubts about our loveability are temporarily suspended. When the honeymoon phase is over – and it could last four weeks or a weekend – then we start to think about the past. At this point we begin to worry and ruminate: 'Where is this going?', 'Is this for real?', 'Could this be true?' This is where feelings of a lack of self-worth or self-sabotage start to kick in.

It's important to recognise that actually there are ways in which many of us make it difficult for people to love us.

And if you really get back to basics, if you are not good at loving yourself, you will accuse others of not loving you. And that's not just in romance, that is across the board in all relationships.

The second statement is true. Loving yourself opens the door to love. It is similar to the unconditional love parents have for their children, or that of true friendships. It is where you love others but without sacrificing aspects of yourself. So now you need to **boost your self-love quotient** in a deceptively simple process. It's important to be willing to make an intentional effort to be more loving to yourself.

In order to do this, Dr Holden says you need to listen to the voice within you that will tell you how you could love yourself more. You have an inner wisdom, an inner voice. So get quiet for a few minutes. Put your hand on your heart, as that's a somatic movement (meaning it relates to the body, as distinct from the mind). Take a deep breath. Connect with your inner-wisdom voice of love. Ask how you can love or admire yourself more today. See if you can find something very practical, very tangible that is a way of loving or admiring yourself today. It could be slowing the pace of your day down, making sure you eat foods that love you, rather than foods that aren't good for you, listening to the intelligence of your body, making sure you don't rush through the whole day and even making sure you include yourself in the day in some way, and it's not only about everybody else. Sometimes you need to come back to who you are. Maybe it's remembering to have a bit of fun.

There is another benefit to this too, as the better we are at loving ourselves, the less pressure everybody else feels to love us – as we are not out-sourcing our self-love to somebody else! Your job is to like yourself and love yourself and if someone else loves you too, that is a BONUS, not the be-all and end-all!

Let's do it now.

> Give yourself five minutes to do this.
>
> - Sit or lie somewhere quiet with no distractions.
>
> - Put your hand on your heart.
>
> - Take a deep breath.
>
> - Ask yourself: 'How can I be loving to myself today?'

Another daily exercise should be to consciously ask yourself: 'How can I make it easier for people to love me?' One of the biggest blocks to love is being 'in a role' in our lives. The role can be things like 'the helper', 'the carer' or 'the responsible one'. Roles block intimacy and they can be polarising. Come out of your role as it limits who you are. Be a better receiver. Ask for help when you need it. When somebody offers to make you a cup of tea, don't say: 'I'm fine, thanks.' Let people in. Let people help you. Tell people how you are.

That role has served you for a chapter of your life. But if you are looking for love, you are looking to start a new chapter now. It's time to relinquish it and redefine who you are too. So ask yourself this question:

How can I pivot?

Can you be agile enough to say: 'OK, I did it that way then, but I'm open to doing this a bit differently now'? You also need to open yourself to an attitude of gratitude. So if someone pays you a compliment, say 'thank you' and don't get defensive or fall over in surprise. If you can start to do that, then you are starting to let people in a bit more.

One last thing ... People often ask Dr Holden about internet dating. His philosophy is *try it*, because when you say yes to doing something you aren't entirely comfortable with, that tells the universe you are more open than before. He also recommends making a list of qualities and values. Many of his clients bumped into someone they fell in love with at their local shop, after they went onto a dating app, as they were more open to possibility. We have our preferred ways of having things happen. But as Dr Holden says: 'With manifesting we have to be open to things happening in delightful and surprising ways.' So, it's fine to have an intention but you need to have an open mind and be adaptable.

The American astrophysicist Carl Sagan once said: 'If you wish to make an apple pie from scratch, you must first invent the universe.' He was effectively saying, if you want to create something 'from scratch' you need to start off with the birth of the universe. We are all part of the universe as the universe has created us, so we've got to be willing to take off our blinkers.

Dr Holden sums it up as: 'In order to manifest love, we have to just say to love: "Over to you." I'm going to say yes to love's plan. But what I am going to do is make sure I'm ready for it as I'm doing the self-love work, I am making it easier for people to love me, I am setting an intention to be a loving person today, I am being present and I'm being the love that I'm looking for.'

RESOLVING CONFLICT

A strategy to address conflict is also key to any functional relationship. The psychologist Marshall Rosenberg was widely considered to be one of the world's leading experts on conflict resolution. His process for this, which he wrote about in his bestselling book *Nonviolent Communication*, involves four steps. This sequence helps you to identify your unmet needs and to express them clearly to your partner, and he/she can do the same.

When the unmet needs have been identified, you can both work towards meeting them and move on. If your partner can't meet those needs, you both now know what your needs are and you can search for other ways to get those needs met.

Here are Rosenberg's four steps to resolving conflict calmly:

1. **Say what you observe.** State what you observe as objectively as possible and avoid being critical or judgemental. This sounds simple but it takes practice because many common words have criticism built into them. For example, 'When I hear you speaking' is neutral. It is not judgemental. However, 'When you criticise me' is itself a critical way of describing the speech. The trick is to find a neutral description. In our earlier example, John could respond to Jane by saying, 'I can hear you're upset.' If you find it difficult to find a neutral description, you could explain that's the case, and apologise that your words may not be the most eloquent but you will do your best.

2. **Say what you feel.** We all need to recognise that our emotions are not controlled by other people. For example, when I say, 'I feel fearful', I am taking responsibility for my own emotions. If I said, 'You make me scared', I would imply you are responsible for my emotions.

3 **State your needs.** Every feeling has an underlying need. If the need is met, I feel better. If the need is not met, the feeling is prompting me to create a strategy to get that need met. John could say, 'I need to feel understood!'

4 **Make your request in a clear way.** John feels really confused, but doesn't know why, so instead of reacting defensively, he could say, 'I need to understand exactly what's upsetting you, so we can stop it happening again.' If Jane can tell him about her need for security and affection, they will soon find common ground.

Now you have begun Power Manifesting **relationships and love**, add it to your internal timeline to set it in action. Now if you wish, you can Power Manifest **health**, more **money** coming into your life, a better **career** or **lifestyle and happiness**. The choice is yours.

BUSINESS MANIFESTOR

British entrepreneur and *The Diary of a CEO* host Steven Bartlett has said: 'I definitely manifested my entire life.' He wrote in his diary at 18 he'd have a six-pack, a girlfriend, a million pounds and a Range Rover within seven years. He achieved it.

Power Manifesting money

Have you ever dreamed of creating more money? This section shows how you can Power Manifest money and dial up your wealth thermostat to enjoy increased abundance. When I recently put a version of this process on the internet it had 450,000 views in just two months!

I created it after I helped an entrepreneur who kept blowing things every time he was on the brink of success. I discovered he'd been told by his mother as a child: 'Son, you don't want to be successful. Successful people have heart attacks.' Those words became embedded in his unconscious mind. It meant throughout his life every time he was on the brink of success his unconscious mind would sabotage it. I hypnotised him back to the point when that limiting belief occurred and we dissolved it, using the block remover in Section One, before using the money manifestor process. He went on to enjoy brilliant business success and wealth!

This technique programs your unconscious mind to attract more wealth, using an NLP strategy to transform your neuro-coding. Everyone has a method where they can visualise the money they have and the amount they expect coming in. Some people see it as a block, a bank statement or even notes fluttering down from the sky, or the energy of a bank transfer or something else. In this technique we will increase the amount coming in, until it almost feels too much. When you do it again and again, that allows you to smash through your limitations. This is because during this process we are talking directly to your unconscious mind telling it to 'go and create this'. It then finds a way to do it!

People who have done this have had astounding changes in their fortune. I recently did it with a friend of mine who went from earning a modest sum to becoming a millionaire within just over a year. His unconscious mind came up with a plan to make it happen!

Doing this will also change your wealth thermostat. As you become richer on the outside you have to become richer on the inside too, otherwise you won't get to keep it. Studies show that around 70 per cent of people who come into a lot of money unexpectedly, through, say, lottery wins or inheritance, blow the lot within a few years. Doing this technique helps to alter your internal thermostat so it's easier for money to come into your life and for you to keep it.

BOOST YOUR WEALTH

🔊 Please read through this technique first, before you do it, or even better click on the audio and I will personally guide you through it.

1. Think about how much money you have in the bank and notice what you imagine. Do you envisage piles of banknotes, stacks of coins, a bank statement or something else?

2. Next, think about how much money you have coming in over the next year and again notice what comes to mind. Do you see cheques, notes, bank statements, envelopes, or numbers going up on your home computer?

3. Now, imagine double, triple or even quadruple the amount of money coming in. You might see more notes piling up, or the numbers on the screen increasing more quickly. Have fun with this!

continued

4. Next, imagine that this flow of wealth increases every year for the next 20 years. Imagine stack after stack of banknotes being added to your account, making the piles bigger and bigger, or watching the numbers on your bank statement dramatically increase. Again, let your imagination run wild and enjoy it!

5. When you are done, let your mind settle on an image that feels expansive and rich to you, making sure that you always finish with more wealth in your mind than you had when you began. It is essential that you allow yourself to enjoy this exercise! By stretching the limits of how much money you can imagine having, you are gradually resetting your wealth thermostat at a higher and higher level.

Now you have Power Manifested money, next, if you wish and haven't already, we can manifest your **health, relationships and love, career** or **lifestyle and happiness**. The power is in your hands to choose to make your life vision even more terrific!

Power Manifesting your dream career

There is a famous saying: 'If you find a job you love you never work again.' So, first, I want to ask you a simple question:

What are you so passionate about you'd pay to do it for a living?

The times when I haven't loved what I was doing in my work and I've pursued something for the wrong reasons, such as chasing money or power, it's always been tainted with unhappiness. So I want you to take a moment and call up your dream career. Now imagine living a day in it. What do you do? How do people treat you? How do you treat them? What are the things you love about it? How does that career make you feel?

I approach my work in a very technical, clinical-based way but I also take great pride in knowing that when I teach someone NLP to use in their own clinical practice, they are going to get so good at it that they are going to affect the lives of thousands of people during their career. As well as the nuts and bolts of NLP, I also install a mindset of curiosity, tenacity and abundance, which in turn gets passed on to their clients. So there is an amazing ripple effect. Knowing I am making a positive difference gives me job satisfaction.

So now I want you to Power Manifest your ultimate career using two powerful Japanese concepts that can give you key insights. If you are already in your dream job, it can also help you find ways to make things even better!

THE CONCEPTS OF *IKIGAI* AND *KAIZEN*

A friend of mine who is a cryptocurrency billionaire lives by the Japanese concept of *ikigai*, which is a recipe for happiness and success. The name merges together two words: '*iki*', which means 'alive', and '*gai*', which means 'reason' – so it's a philosophy about what gives your career (and ultimately your life) reason, meaning and purpose. It is said to be a way of life on the islands of Okinawa in Japan, where people are famed for their longevity.

Ikigai is based around four pillars of: **What do you love? What are you good at? What can you get paid for? What do you bring to the world that it needs?** These four areas are key to bringing you clarity on your life's purpose. There are four overlapping circles in the *ikigai* graphic below, each of which contains one of the pillars. When some people fill in the four circles they may find their career is not aligned with their purpose. So, for instance, you may be doing a job solely for the money. Now for some, earning cash is their purpose as it enables them to provide for their loved ones. For others, they may feel less fulfilment or job satisfaction.

Everyone is different. The key to this is when you fill in each of the circles you suddenly get clarity about what is important to you in life. Many people also get key insights about themselves when they fill in what they bring to the world. This is not about status or money; it is about your unique values and what you bring as an individual. The idea behind it is that when you fill in the circles you will feel a real sense of your purpose and what your mission in life is. Interestingly, my friend's take is that when you align these four areas, then money and fulfilment will also find you.

I once helped someone who worked in the civil service who felt totally unfulfilled. He would turn up to work on a Monday morning and his colleagues would say: 'Roll on retirement!' When he told me this story I said, 'What was it like?' He replied: 'It was the most soul-destroying place.' He ended up leaving and embarking on a career that gave him job satisfaction – and he earned a lot more money as a result. This is because people who follow their passions, missions and vocation in their profession are often very successful.

My crypto friend has plenty of money but, as he explained it, the cash is a side effect of living by the power of *ikigai*.

When I filled in the circles I found the following: What do I love? *Hypnosis!* What am I good at? *Hypnosis!* What can I get paid for? *Hypnosis!* What do I bring to the world? *Hypnosis!* It confirmed to me that I am following a path of fulfilling my life's purpose.

What I also love about this way of working is that you are not seeking perfection. *Ikigai* aims for 80 per cent completeness, so you don't exhaust yourself chasing unattainable goals.

Remember, in order to find your *ikigai* you need to fill in the four circles in the diagram. Once you do this, one of two things will happen. The first is that the career you should consider will become apparent to you. Or, if you are already doing what you should be, once you have filled in your *ikigai* circles and have them aligned, your career will get better. If they are not aligned you may be chasing after something you think will make you happy, which generally is pleasure or money, or it may be a short-lived fix that does not ultimately fulfil you. You may also decide to have a job that may not necessarily completely fulfil you, but to have passions that bridge the gap. If so, add your hobbies to the circles as well. Let's do it now.

I also live by the concept of *kaizen*, which is also an amalgamation of two other Japanese terms: '*kai*' meaning 'change' and '*zen*' meaning 'constant, never-ending improvement'. This business philosophy is used to this day by Toyota. So no matter what you've got, or where you are, the philosophy is that you try to improve it.

Kaizen was first practised in Japanese businesses after World War II. The story goes that after their factories were bombed out, they decided that one day they'd sweep up one corner and the next they'd do something else. Each day they'd ask: 'What could we do today to make things better?' So at its core is incremental improvements. This is relevant to our work as well as our personal wellbeing. While it started as a post-war concept, I'd argue that in our digital world, where we are continually bombarded with images of people's seemingly perfect lives, this has never been more relevant. Stop comparing yourself to others. Only compare yourself to yourself. So ask yourself each day, are you doing one little thing to make your life better? That's a really functional mindset that I try to live by. In the journal at the back of this guide is a space where you can write the one thing you've done to make your life better every day.

Now you have Power Manifested your career, add it to your internal timeline. If you haven't done so already, you may now choose to add **health, relationships and love, money** or **lifestyle and happiness** to ramp up your life even more!

HOLLYWOOD MANIFESTOR

Actress Jennifer Aniston recently revealed on *The Drew Barrymore Show* that she is a manifestor. She said: 'I've been told to manifest whatever it is you are wanting to manifest; you speak to it as though it's already happened.'

Power Manifesting your lifestyle and happiness

There is a Chinese proverb that says if you want to be happy for an hour take a walk; if you want to be happy for a week take a holiday; if you want to be happy for a year win the lottery; and if you want to be happy for the rest of your life, help other people.

For me, lifestyle is about balance. This is something that I still struggle with at times, but I'm much better at it than I used to be. I used to be a workaholic. I would fly to Sydney, Australia, get off the plane, go and do some TV and radio interviews, go out with a publisher, then fly to Melbourne, do the same again and fly back to England, without stopping to catch a breath! So I had not fed my soul. A few years ago I had an event in Eastern Europe and I asked Kate, 'Why are we going a day earlier and staying later?' She replied, 'Because we are going to have some "me time" after work!' So I didn't just have business, I had fun and enjoyed the culture too!

Feeding your soul can be as simple as spending time with your children, family or friends and experiencing the joy and memories it brings. So now my lifestyle is focused on a balance of work, helping others and the things I want to do for pleasure, fun or relaxation.

When focusing on your lifestyle, it's important to also differentiate between being overwhelmed and overloaded. We overwhelm ourselves by stacking things one on top of another in our minds. Overwhelm is psychological. You could get overwhelmed over not being able to find your socks. It's not that it's actually a difficult activity, although it can lead you to rail against the world and the washing machine sock-eating monster. Overload is where there actually is too much on your plate. If you have a feeling that you can't do what you need to do, then you need to create an A B C list, which will give you a strategy to manage when you have too many plates spinning at once. In your list, A's are things that have to be done immediately, or there's trouble or a consequence. B's are things that are important but can wait. Everything else is a C.

Now you have a strategy to prioritise, I'd like you to visualise living a series of perfect days. These days need to be filled with love, happiness, optimism and creativity – which are all high-frequency states. Imagine living a perfect day at home, a perfect day with a loved one and a perfect day on holiday. Choose as many perfect days as you wish. Have fun with it! See yourself living them and looking happy and healthy as if they have already happened.

The reason I want you to choose a day is that it has a beginning and an end. When you know something is finite, you treat it completely differently to something you think is infinite. So if you knew you were going to live forever you would approach life completely differently. Endings, in a sense, can be empowering as they can organise your thinking and behaviour. There is a saying often attributed to the Buddha: 'The problem is they think they have time.' When you put it like that, it puts everything into perspective. Life is so short you need to make sure you are with the right people doing the right things, in good health, and getting as much joy as possible.

I used to view success as money, fame and power. My perspective has changed, as there's no end to that. It is insatiable. Now you have Power Manifested your lifestyle through your perfect days, add them to your internal timeline in order to set them in motion.

Whether you have done one, two or all of the techniques in Section Three you are now an Advanced Power

Manifestor. You have taken the keys to manifest not only your dreams, but also those key areas of your life. Please continue to use these techniques to continue to create a better life for yourself, as the more you Power Manifest, the better your life will get.

Returning to your baseline

You are almost at the end of this book. Your future is bigger, bolder, brighter and more expansive than you ever thought possible before. So it is time to return to your baseline (see overleaf). First, remember all the wonderful things you have added to your internal timeline and what you have already Power Manifested with the clarity and insights you have gained. This reinforces this process and makes you aware of what you have already achieved.

Take a few moments to do this now. Now I want you to take a reading for your life in the knowledge that amazing things are unfolding.

- On a scale from 1 to 10, if you continue on the path to manifesting the life you want, how do you suspect you'll rate your **health** in one year and then five years from now?

- On a scale from 1 to 10, how would you rate your **relationships and love** if you continue on this path in one year and then five years from now?

- On a scale from 1 to 10, how would you rate your **money and finances** if you continue on this path in one year and five years from now?

- On a scale from 1 to 10, how would you rate your **career** if you continue on this path in one year and five years from now?

- On a scale from 1 to 10, how would you rate your **lifestyle and happiness** in one year and five years if you continue to manifest your life from now?

MUSIC MANIFESTOR

International pop star Ariana Grande has said: 'My mum always taught me that if I want something it can happen. To never act like it's not. I think, in a way, that's manifestation.'

Embrace your amazing new future

Congratulations, you have now harnessed the power of Power Manifesting, and if you chose to do Section Three you will also be an Advanced Power Manifestor. You will already have a sense of control over your life and where you are going. Your future is now safe in your hands. You are no longer a victim of circumstance, but instead you are a master of your own destiny.

This is the beginning of a great adventure for you. Over the coming months, your dreams will start to be realised and you will notice evidence of it happening. So start writing down the things you manifest or the serendipities that happen. For instance, if you have manifested money, even if you find a pound coin, write it down. If you have manifested love, when a good-looking person smiles at you, or responds to you differently, write that down too. Also write down anything about the way you act or feel when it comes to matters of the heart. It affirms in your mind a glass-half-full mindset, which in turn will boost your frequency.

I always remember once treating someone, many years ago, for insomnia. He came to see me two weeks later and I said: 'How is it?' and he replied: 'I'm not cured.' I said: 'How much better are you?' His answer was: 'Eighty per cent.' His experience illustrates how sometimes success is right before our eyes, but we still don't see it. That's why noticing the small things is so powerful and important. It plays a big part in keeping the momentum going. Remember Power Manifesting is a way of life – so you need to *live it*. I call it 'listening for the whispers' as they're what show you change is underway.

Every day I recommend you focus on your dream or new life vision using the Five Minutes of Focus technique (see page 78). That's all it takes. Quieten your mind, call up your vision from your timeline, focus on what you need to do next to get there and visualise just how brilliant it's going to be. Remember, see it as though you are already living it. You can do this focus time in increments to make up five minutes if that works better for you. Try to do it every day. This tells your unconscious: 'My life is moving in this direction. This is happening.' That makes it more likely to happen. At any point you can also return to the techniques in this book to reaffirm your vision, or add a new dream so that you can make that happen too.

For a proportion of people there will be a eureka moment where their life changes in an instant. Others need to reinforce it so that they keep moving towards their dream. At times, you might suffer a setback. But if you know where you are going things will ultimately work out. Remember the aeroplane flying through the sky. Winds may blow it slightly off course for a bit of the flight, or you may have a slight detour for other air traffic, but ultimately that plane knows its destination. As long as you know where you are headed you can compensate for deviations. Remember, this is just the beginning ... your new better, brighter future is now in your hands.

Until we meet. Paul.

Daily Power Manifesting and Gratitude Journal

What gets measured gets done. When you make a record of something you are more likely to accomplish it. It's like having training wheels on a bike. It initially keeps you on course and eventually you take the training wheels off and it has become a habit.

This is one of the smallest things that makes the biggest difference. If you do this every day, remembering the Five Minutes of Focus, there is no way that things aren't going to get better.

DAILY POWER MANIFESTATION

1. Have you focused on manifesting great **health** today?

2. Have you focused on manifesting wonderful **relationships and love** today?

3. Have you focused on manifesting **money** today?

4. Have you focused on manifesting a fabulous **career** today?

5. Have you focused on manifesting the **lifestyle and happiness** that you want today?

Keeping a gratitude journal

One of the simplest and most powerful things you can do to elevate the baseline of your mood is a daily gratitude journal. It really struck me how well this process worked during the pandemic, when people I knew who were feeling a bit low simply made a list of everything they were grateful for and it gave them a fresh perspective. You can write down big things like health, friends and family, or small things like the first cup of tea or coffee in the morning.

When you start to consider all the things that you feel grateful for, you are reinforcing in your mind things that make you feel great. As you already know from this book, we get more of what we focus on, so you are training your brain to focus on and search out things that improve your mood. It takes just a few minutes to do each day and then if you are feeling a bit low, just read back through your lists and you will start to feel better.

As with any new habit, you have to push yourself to do it the first few times and then, as momentum builds, it becomes second nature. That's why the gratitude journal runs for

30 days. All you have to do is make a note of ten things that you feel grateful for – it can be the same or similar every day because the point is to elicit positive feelings connected to your life and reinforce those feelings. You remember how we become hardwired through what we continually think about? That's how this approach to journalling works.

Also, it's vitally important to foster a sense of purpose in life. The legendary psychiatrist and Holocaust survivor Viktor Frankl famously said, 'Purpose is the cornerstone of good mental health.' Your purpose is not necessarily your job, although your work is likely to be a part of your purpose. While manifesting **money** is one of the most popular techniques, you have got to have your **health, relationships and love, career, lifestyle and happiness** and things to look forward to, too. Bob Marley once said: 'Some people are so poor, all they have is money.'

What I've discovered after 40 years in the trenches working with people is that if you don't get a balance in these areas of your life you are likely to end up unhappy. You may also wish to add others, including spirituality for instance. A purpose can be being a good spouse, or a big thing like being a force for good in the world, or it could simply be to strive to be the best version of yourself.

I worked with a guy who achieved an extraordinary amount in the world but he was suffering from burnout. He said to me: 'I'm lost.' I said, 'You have got to find purpose.' He started small. Initially, he told me, 'I got some orchids, I get up each morning and my purpose that day was not to run my empire but just to tend to the orchids.' He went back to small to rebuild as he had burned himself out. And now he's chosen to run his international empire again.

A friend of mine who became a billionaire was never motivated by money. His purpose was always that he wanted to touch a billion souls in a positive way through his work. He has been a pivotal figure in the development of a vaccine that is set to change the world. He always says: 'Only people who have touched a billion souls should be able to say they are billionaires.' I love that ethos.

My smaller purpose each morning is to make the best cup of tea. I make one for my wife Kate and one for me. It's an act of service I love to do for my wife. But if I am thinking BIG, well, I want to change the world through hypnotherapy and train more hypnotherapists than anyone else on this planet. If I train all these people they will change the lives of countless others and that's how you can ultimately end up touching a billion souls.

So, also on your gratitude list, it is really important for you to state your purpose. You may have more than one. It may also be your purpose for that day, that week or indeed your life. I cannot emphasise enough how powerful this process is. Here's an example of my gratitude list for a day.

1. Health, mental/physical.
2. Family.
3. Friends.
4. A happy home.
5. My work.
6. First cup of tea in the morning.
7. A TV show I am looking forward to watching.
8. Where I live in the world.
9. Food and wine.
10. Clean water.

MY PURPOSE:

- To be a good husband and friend.
- To be creative.
- To help others.
- To have success in my career.

Now it's your turn. Set aside a time each day to write down what you are grateful for and make sure to re-read your list regularly. This is a small thing that makes such a big difference I have put it in several of my books. I cannot stress enough the benefits of doing this.

POWER MANIFESTING

DAY 1

Today I am grateful for…

1. _____
2. _____
3. _____
4. _____
5. _____
6. _____
7. _____
8. _____
9. _____
10. _____

My purpose for today is:

Time spent focused (minutes): _____

DAY 2

Today I am grateful for...

1. _____
2. _____
3. _____
4. _____
5. _____
6. _____
7. _____
8. _____
9. _____
10. _____

My purpose for today is:

```



```

Time spent focused (minutes): _____

DAY 3

Today I am grateful for…

1. _____
2. _____
3. _____
4. _____
5. _____
6. _____
7. _____
8. _____
9. _____
10. _____

My purpose for today is:

```
┌─────────────────────────────────┐
│                                 │
│                                 │
│                                 │
│                                 │
└─────────────────────────────────┘
```

Time spent focused (minutes): _____

DAILY POWER MANIFESTING AND GRATITUDE JOURNAL

DAY 4

Today I am grateful for...

1. _____
2. _____
3. _____
4. _____
5. _____
6. _____
7. _____
8. _____
9. _____
10. _____

My purpose for today is:

Time spent focused (minutes): _____

DAY 5

Today I am grateful for...

1. _____
2. _____
3. _____
4. _____
5. _____
6. _____
7. _____
8. _____
9. _____
10. _____

My purpose for today is:

Time spent focused (minutes): _____

DAY 6

Today I am grateful for...

1. _____
2. _____
3. _____
4. _____
5. _____
6. _____
7. _____
8. _____
9. _____
10. _____

My purpose for today is:

Time spent focused (minutes): _____

DAY 7

Today I am grateful for...

1. _____
2. _____
3. _____
4. _____
5. _____
6. _____
7. _____
8. _____
9. _____
10. _____

My purpose for today is:

_____

Time spent focused (minutes): _____

DAILY POWER MANIFESTING AND GRATITUDE JOURNAL

DAY 8

Today I am grateful for...

1. _____
2. _____
3. _____
4. _____
5. _____
6. _____
7. _____
8. _____
9. _____
10. _____

My purpose for today is:

```
┌─────────────────────────────────────────┐
│                                         │
│                                         │
│                                         │
│                                         │
└─────────────────────────────────────────┘
```

Time spent focused (minutes): _____

DAY 9

Today I am grateful for…

1. _____
2. _____
3. _____
4. _____
5. _____
6. _____
7. _____
8. _____
9. _____
10. _____

My purpose for today is:

Time spent focused (minutes): _____

DAY 10

Today I am grateful for…

1. _____
2. _____
3. _____
4. _____
5. _____
6. _____
7. _____
8. _____
9. _____
10. _____

My purpose for today is:

Time spent focused (minutes): _____

DAY 11

Today I am grateful for...

1. _____
2. _____
3. _____
4. _____
5. _____
6. _____
7. _____
8. _____
9. _____
10. _____

My purpose for today is:

Time spent focused (minutes): _____

DAY 12

Today I am grateful for…

1. _____
2. _____
3. _____
4. _____
5. _____
6. _____
7. _____
8. _____
9 _____
10. _____

My purpose for today is:

Time spent focused (minutes): _____

DAY 13

Today I am grateful for…

1. _____
2. _____
3. _____
4. _____
5. _____
6. _____
7. _____
8. _____
9. _____
10. _____

My purpose for today is:

Time spent focused (minutes): _____

DAY 14

Today I am grateful for…

1. _____
2. _____
3. _____
4. _____
5. _____
6. _____
7. _____
8. _____
9. _____
10. _____

My purpose for today is:

Time spent focused (minutes): _____

DAY 15

Today I am grateful for...

1. _____
2. _____
3. _____
4. _____
5. _____
6. _____
7. _____
8. _____
9. _____
10. _____

My purpose for today is:

Time spent focused (minutes): _____

DAY 16

Today I am grateful for…

1. _____
2. _____
3. _____
4. _____
5. _____
6. _____
7. _____
8. _____
9. _____
10. _____

My purpose for today is:

```
┌─────────────────────────────────────────┐
│                                         │
│                                         │
│                                         │
│                                         │
└─────────────────────────────────────────┘
```

Time spent focused (minutes): _____

DAY 17

Today I am grateful for...

1. _____
2. _____
3. _____
4. _____
5. _____
6. _____
7. _____
8. _____
9. _____
10. _____

My purpose for today is:

Time spent focused (minutes): _____

DAY 18

Today I am grateful for...

1. _____
2. _____
3. _____
4. _____
5. _____
6. _____
7. _____
8. _____
9. _____
10. _____

My purpose for today is:

Time spent focused (minutes): _____

POWER MANIFESTING

DAY 19

Today I am grateful for...

1. _____
2. _____
3. _____
4. _____
5. _____
6. _____
7. _____
8. _____
9. _____
10. _____

My purpose for today is:

Time spent focused (minutes): _____

DAY 20

Today I am grateful for...

1. _____
2. _____
3. _____
4. _____
5. _____
6. _____
7. _____
8. _____
9. _____
10. _____

My purpose for today is:

Time spent focused (minutes): _____

DAY 21

Today I am grateful for…

1. _____
2. _____
3. _____
4. _____
5. _____
6. _____
7. _____
8. _____
9. _____
10. _____

My purpose for today is:

Time spent focused (minutes): _____

DAILY POWER MANIFESTING AND GRATITUDE JOURNAL

DAY 22

Today I am grateful for…

1. _____
2. _____
3. _____
4. _____
5. _____
6. _____
7. _____
8. _____
9. _____
10. _____

My purpose for today is:

Time spent focused (minutes): _____

DAY 23

Today I am grateful for…

1. _____
2. _____
3. _____
4. _____
5. _____
6. _____
7. _____
8. _____
9. _____
10. _____

My purpose for today is:

Time spent focused (minutes): _____

DAY 24

Today I am grateful for...

1. _____
2. _____
3. _____
4. _____
5. _____
6. _____
7. _____
8. _____
9 _____
10. _____

My purpose for today is:

Time spent focused (minutes): _____

DAY 25

Today I am grateful for…

1. _____
2. _____
3. _____
4. _____
5. _____
6. _____
7. _____
8. _____
9. _____
10. _____

My purpose for today is:

Time spent focused (minutes): _____

DAY 26

Today I am grateful for...

1. _____
2. _____
3. _____
4. _____
5. _____
6. _____
7. _____
8. _____
9. _____
10. _____

My purpose for today is:

Time spent focused (minutes): _____

DAY 27

Today I am grateful for...

1. _____
2. _____
3. _____
4. _____
5. _____
6. _____
7. _____
8. _____
9. _____
10. _____

My purpose for today is:

Time spent focused (minutes): _____

DAY 28

Today I am grateful for...

1. _____
2. _____
3. _____
4. _____
5. _____
6. _____
7. _____
8. _____
9. _____
10. _____

My purpose for today is:

Time spent focused (minutes): _____

DAY 29

Today I am grateful for...

1. _____
2. _____
3. _____
4. _____
5. _____
6. _____
7. _____
8. _____
9. _____
10. _____

My purpose for today is:

Time spent focused (minutes): _____

DAY 30

Today I am grateful for...

1. _____
2. _____
3. _____
4. _____
5. _____
6. _____
7. _____
8. _____
9. _____
10. _____

My purpose for today is:

Time spent focused (minutes): _____

One thing to make your life better each day

Finally, remember to write each day one thing you've done to make your life better. It can be big or small. It can be asking yourself: 'Have I been creative, laughed, done a random act of kindness, did I do an act of self-care? Did I take one tiny step towards achieving a goal that I want? Did I do an act of service for my partner to make them smile?'

Now it's your turn.

ONE THING I'VE DONE TODAY:

DAY 1:

DAY 2:

DAILY POWER MANIFESTING AND GRATITUDE JOURNAL

DAY 3:

DAY 4:

DAY 5:

DAY 6:

DAY 7:

POWER MANIFESTING

DAY 8:

DAY 9:

DAY 10:

DAY 11:

DAY 12:

DAY 13:

DAY 14:

DAY 15:

DAY 16:

DAY 17:

POWER MANIFESTING

DAY 18:

DAY 19:

DAY 20:

DAY 21:

DAY 22:

DAILY POWER MANIFESTING AND GRATITUDE JOURNAL

DAY 23:

DAY 24:

DAY 25:

DAY 26:

DAY 27:

POWER MANIFESTING

DAY 28:

DAY 29:

DAY 30:

MUSIC MANIFESTOR

Pop star Lizzo revealed at the MTV VMAs in 2019 that she was a manifestor. She said: 'Dreams do come true and you truly can manifest your reality.'

Further reading

Dr Richard Bandler, *Get the Life You Want* (Harper Element, 2009)

Professor Robert A. Emmons, *Gratitude Works!* (Jossey-Bass, 2013)

Dr Robert Holden, *Loveability* (Hay House, 2013)

Dr Bruce Lipton, *The Biology of Belief* (Hay House, 2016)

Professor Gloria Mark, *Attention Span* (William Collins, 2023)

Dr Dean Radin, *The Conscious Universe* (HarperOne, 2009)

Dr Ronald Ruden, *The Craving Brain* (Harper Perennial, 2000)

Dr Stephen Simpson, *The Psychoic Revolution* (independently published, 2018)

Dr Richard Wiseman, *The Luck Factor* (Arrow, 2004)

Jack M. Zufelt, *The DNA of Success* (HarperCollins, 2002)

Acknowledgements

My thanks to Sarah Arnold, Neil Reading, Ben Hasler, Mike Osborne, Oliver Holden-Rea, Lindsay Davies, Alex Clarke, Steve Shaw, Caroline Michel and Alex Tuppen.

Also, a special thank you to my wife Kate McKenna.

Index of techniques

SECTION ONE:
THE FOUNDATIONS OF POWER MANIFESTING

Step One: Healing the Younger You **30**

Step Two: Stepping into the New You **33**

The Frequency Booster **48**

Get into the Authenticity Zone **53**

Getting Clean and Clear **58**

The Core Desire Scale **61**

Ecology Checks **62**

The Block Remover **66**

Your Five Dreams **69**

SECTION TWO:
POWER MANIFESTING IN ACTION

The Power of Five Minutes of Focus **78**

Upside/Downside **88**

Harness Your Intuition **95**

The Luck Generator **103**

Harness Your Internal Timeline **116**

INDEX OF TECHNIQUES

SECTION THREE: ADVANCED POWER MANIFESTING

The Power of Your Karma 132

Using the Power of Your Neuro-Coding 137

Power Manifesting Health 138

Power Manifesting Relationships and Love 146

Power Manifesting Money 171

Power Manifesting Your Dream Career 175

The Concepts of *Ikigai* and *Kaizen* 176

Power Manifesting Your Lifestyle and Happiness 183

Returning to Your Baseline 187

Notes

Notes

About the author

PAUL MCKENNA, Ph.D. was recently named by the *London Times* as one of the world's leading modern gurus alongside Nelson Mandela and the Dalai Lama. He is Britain's bestselling non-fiction author, selling over 15 million books in 35 countries around the world. He has worked his unique brand of personal transformation with Hollywood movie stars, Olympic gold medalists, rock stars, leading business achievers and royalty. Over the past 40 years, Paul McKenna has helped millions of people successfully quit smoking, lose weight, overcome insomnia, eliminate stress, and increase self-confidence. Paul McKenna is regularly watched on TV by hundreds of millions of people in 42 countries around the world. He now runs the world's number-one hypnotherapy training organisation with Mindvalley.